Building D Teamwork in Schools

How can school leaders foster more effective teamwork and collaboration among teachers to improve instruction and culture? Brad Johnson and Robert Hinchliffe use the analogy of geese V formations to show what effective teamwork really looks like for success. He discusses roles and responsibilities – each goose has a role to play in the flock, from leader to follower; the importance of recognizing individual strengths and assigning roles accordingly; and the impact of each team member fulfilling their responsibilities. He also discusses the skills that the teams need in order to work together: working together to achieve a common goal; fostering a sense of unity and shared purpose; adaptability and flexibility; encouragement and support; trust and reliance; and leadership and followership. Each chapter is filled with strategies and examples for leaders in any setting and ends with a Sharpen Your Winning Edge section offering tips you can use immediately.

Brad Johnson (@DrBradJohnson) has over 25 years of experience as a teacher and administrator at the K–12 and collegiate level. He is the author of several books and one of the most inspirational and affirmational speakers in education.

Robert Hinchliffe is a successful principal in Las Vegas, Nevada, and has been an administrator for over 18 years. He is the author of the book *It's All About Perspective* and hosts a podcast with the same name.

Also Available from Brad Johnson &
Routledge Eye On Education
www.routledge.com/k-12

Becoming a More Assertive Teacher:
Maximizing Strengths, Establishing Boundaries, and
Amplifying Your Voice

Dear School Leader:
50 Motivational Quotes and Anecdotes that Affirm Your
Purpose and Your Impact

Dear Teacher:
100 Days of Inspirational Quotes and Anecdotes
with Hal Bowman

Thank You, Teacher:
100 Uplifting and Affirming Letters from Your Fellow Educators
with Hal Bowman

Principal Bootcamp:
Accelerated Strategies to Influence and Lead from Day One

Putting Teachers First:
How to Inspire, Motivate, and Connect with Your Staff

Learning On Your Feet, 2e:
Incorporating Physical Activity into the K-8 Classroom
with Melody Jones

What Schools Don't Teach:
20 Ways to Help Students Excel in School and in Life
Brad Johnson and Julie Sessions

From School Administrator to School Leader:
15 Keys to Maximizing Your Leadership Potential
Brad Johnson and Julie Sessions

Building Dynamic Teamwork in Schools

12 Principles of the V Formation to Transform Culture

Brad Johnson and Robert Hinchliffe

Routledge
Taylor & Francis Group

NEW YORK AND LONDON

Designed cover image: © Getty Images

First published 2024
by Routledge
605 Third Avenue, New York, NY 10158

and by Routledge
4 Park Square, Milton Park, Abingdon, Oxon, OX14 4RN

Routledge is an imprint of the Taylor & Francis Group, an informa business

© 2024 Brad Johnson and Robert Hinchliffe

The right of Brad Johnson and Robert Hinchliffe to be identified as authors of this work has been asserted in accordance with sections 77 and 78 of the Copyright, Designs and Patents Act 1988.

All rights reserved. No part of this book may be reprinted or reproduced or utilised in any form or by any electronic, mechanical, or other means, now known or hereafter invented, including photocopying and recording, or in any information storage or retrieval system, without permission in writing from the publishers.

Trademark notice: Product or corporate names may be trademarks or registered trademarks, and are used only for identification and explanation without intent to infringe.

Library of Congress Cataloging-in-Publication Data
Names: Johnson, Brad, 1969– author. | Hinchliff, Robert, author.
Title: Building dynamic teamwork in schools : 12 principles of the V
    formation to transform culture / Brad Johnson and Robert Hinchliff.
Description: New York, NY : Routledge, 2023. | Includes
    bibliographical references.
Identifiers: LCCN 2023033844 (print) | LCCN 2023033845 (ebook) |
    ISBN 9781032592503 (paperback) | ISBN 9781032592510 (hardback) |
    ISBN 9781003453819 (ebook)
Subjects: LCSH: School management and organization. | Educational
    leadership. | Teacher-administrator relationships. |
    Teachers—Professional relationships.
Classification: LCC LB2805 .J6359 2023 (print) | LCC LB2805 (ebook) |
    DDC 371.2—dc23/eng/20230913
LC record available at https://lccn.loc.gov/2023033844
LC ebook record available at https://lccn.loc.gov/2023033845

ISBN: 978-1-032-59251-0 (hbk)
ISBN: 978-1-032-59250-3 (pbk)
ISBN: 978-1-003-45381-9 (ebk)

DOI: 10.4324/9781003453819

Typeset in Palatino
by Apex Covantage, LLC

Contents

Introduction

Just like the magnificent sight of geese in flight, the power of synergy within a team of educators is truly awe-inspiring. Geese flying in a V formation not only showcase the remarkable benefits of collaboration and teamwork but also serve as a profound metaphor for the untapped potential within educational teams.

When educators unite as a cohesive team, their collective force becomes an unstoppable phenomenon, akin to the soaring geese. Individually, each bird flapping its wings creates an uplift for the bird following behind, allowing them to achieve greater distances and endurance. Similarly, in the world of education, when educators come together, their combined knowledge, skills, and perspectives create a vibrant tapestry of expertise.

This synergy within the team leads to elevated problem-solving abilities, innovative teaching strategies, and ultimately improved outcomes for students. It is through the harmonious collaboration and shared vision of educators that true greatness can be achieved. By harnessing the collective power of their team, educators can tap into each other's strengths, support one another during challenges, and collaborate to develop highly effective instructional approaches tailored to meet the diverse needs of their students.

But the power of synergy extends beyond academic excellence. When educators seamlessly collaborate, they model the values of teamwork and cooperation for their students, creating a positive and supportive learning environment. This environment fosters a sense of belonging, encourages active participation, and empowers students to develop their own collaborative skills that will serve them well throughout their lives.

This book delves deep into the profound lessons we can learn from geese and offers practical strategies to harness the

DOI: 10.4324/9781003453819-1

power of synergy within educational teams. Through compelling narratives, real-life examples, and actionable steps, this book navigates the intricacies of collaboration, trust-building, and effective communication needed to cultivate highly effective teams.

Together, let us draw inspiration from the geese that grace our skies, recognizing the immense potential that lies within the collective strength of educators. By aligning our talents, uniting our visions, and embracing the diversity within our teams, we can elevate the educational experience to unimaginable heights.

Join us on this transformative journey as we unlock the true power that emerges when we soar together as a team, creating a brighter future for our students and schools. Thank you for embarking on this inspiring journey with us.

1

Principle 1: Harnessing the Power of Teamwork: Lessons from the Geese

One of my favorite times of the year is fall, even if it is short-lived here in the south, where we often transition straight from the heat and humidity of summer to mild winters. Nonetheless, I love the feel of fall. The changing leaves, the crisp air, and the promise of cooler days ahead bring a sense of anticipation and tranquility.

As the days grow shorter and the nights longer, nature undergoes its own transformation. The sky becomes a canvas for migrating birds, a symphony of wings and honks that signal the changing of seasons. And leading this avian migration spectacle are the geese.

I always know winter is on the way when I hear the geese flying over my home. I enjoy sitting out on the deck and listening for them, their honks echoing through the air. Then, like clockwork, they appear, emerging from the distant horizon in their V formations. It's a sight that never fails to captivate me.

Depending on the size of the V formation, the noise can be quite loud and heard from a considerable distance before the geese come into view. But regardless of the size of the group, there are certain characteristics that stand out, such as their distinct V formation and the continuous honking.

DOI: 10.4324/9781003453819-2

As I observe these geese in flight, I am reminded of the remarkable teamwork and cooperation that define their migration patterns. They possess a set of traits that allow them to work together effectively, traits that we as humans can learn from and apply to our own teams and collaborations.

Geese are not just beautiful creatures in flight; they are nature's ambassadors of teamwork. Each honk, each flap of their wings, tells a story of successful cooperation. And as I marvel at their synchronized flight, I can't help but draw parallels to the principles of successful teamwork outlined in the article I recently read.

Communication is key. Geese communicate frequently while in flight, honking to stay connected. Just as team members need to communicate effectively to ensure everyone is on the same page, the geese demonstrate the importance of keeping the lines of communication open.

Leadership takes many forms. Geese take turns leading the flock, with others supporting from behind. In teams, it's crucial to recognize that leadership can be shared, allowing everyone to contribute to the group's success. It's not just about one individual leading the way; it's about collective guidance.

Cooperation fuels progress. Geese work together to achieve a common goal, often rotating positions to conserve energy. In teams, members can cooperate and support each other, recognizing that their collective effort is greater than the sum of individual contributions.

Trust binds the flock. Geese have a sense of trust in their flock, which allows them to follow their leader without hesitation. In teams, trust is essential to establish open communication, foster cooperation, and achieve shared objectives.

Empathy strengthens bonds. Geese show empathy toward one another, waiting for sick or injured geese to catch up to the flock. In teams, empathy can create a more supportive and understanding environment, enhancing collaboration and overall well-being.

Motivation keeps spirits high. Geese encourage each other to keep going, honking to maintain energy levels. In teams, positive motivation can help keep everyone focused and energized, even in challenging times.

Adaptability is the key to survival. Geese adapt their flight path according to weather and obstacles, demonstrating flexibility in achieving their goal. In teams, flexibility and adaptability are essential qualities to overcome unexpected challenges and achieve success.

Diversity breeds innovation. Geese flock together with different ages, genders, and breeds, demonstrating diversity. In teams, embracing diversity can lead to more creativity, fresh perspectives, and greater success in tackling complex problems.

Persistence propels progress. Geese are persistent in reaching their destination, often flying long distances to do so. In teams, persistence is vital in the face of adversity, driving continued efforts toward achieving shared goals.

Recognition fosters a positive environment. Geese celebrate their successes when they reach their destination, often with a vocal display. In teams, recognizing and celebrating achievements can help foster a positive environment, boost morale, and encourage continued success.

As I take in the honking sky above me, I am reminded that the geese's teamwork traits are a testament to the power of collaboration, reminding us of our own potential when we come together. Inspired by their example, I hope you feel a sense of purpose and determination to apply these principles with your own team, knowing that together you can achieve remarkable things as well.

The Power of Collaboration: Why a Team of Teachers Outshines a Group

When you compare a team of teachers to a mere group of teachers, you'll quickly notice the advantages of the former. Here are some compelling reasons why a team of teachers outshines a group:

1. Collaboration: As a team of teachers, you actively collaborate and work together toward common goals. You share ideas, expertise, and resources, engaging in regular discussions and planning sessions. This collaborative

approach allows the pooling of knowledge and the development of comprehensive strategies to meet the needs of all students. In contrast, as individuals in a group of teachers, you may work individually or in isolation, resulting in fragmented efforts and limited coordination.

2. Shared Responsibility: You share the responsibility for student learning and success. Together, you analyze student data, identify areas for improvement, and develop strategies to address challenges. Each team member contributes their unique skills and perspectives, ensuring a more comprehensive and well-rounded approach to instruction. In a group of teachers, the responsibility may be divided or assigned on an individual basis, leading to inconsistent or incomplete support for students.

3. Professional Learning: You provide each other with opportunities for ongoing professional learning and growth. You engage in collaborative professional development activities, such as joint planning, peer observations, and lesson study. This shared learning fosters a culture of continuous improvement and encourages the adoption of effective instructional practices. In a group of teachers, professional learning may be more ad-hoc or individualized, lacking the benefits of collective knowledge and support.

4. Accountability and Feedback: A team of teachers, you establish a system of accountability and feedback within your collaborative framework. You regularly review student progress, evaluate instructional strategies, and provide constructive feedback to one another. This accountability promotes reflection and improvement, ensuring that instructional practices are constantly refined to better meet student needs. In a group of teachers, individual accountability and feedback may be less structured or inconsistent.

5. Resource Utilization: You optimize the use of resources within the school. You coordinate your efforts to effectively allocate time, materials, and other resources based on student needs. This collaborative approach helps maximize the impact of available resources and minimizes duplication or

wastage. Conversely, in a group of teachers, resource utilization may be more fragmented or based on individual preferences, leading to inefficient use of resources.

6. Enhanced Support Systems: Moreover, as a team, you provide a stronger support system for both students and teachers. You can identify struggling students early, develop intervention strategies, and provide targeted support. Additionally, you share the workload, support each other in managing classroom challenges, and offer emotional support. While individual support systems may exist within a group of teachers, they may lack the collective expertise and coordinated approach of a team.

A team of teachers is more effective than a group of teachers because of their emphasis on collaboration, shared responsibility, ongoing professional learning, accountability, efficient resource utilization, and enhanced support systems. By working together, you can leverage your collective strengths and expertise to improve student learning outcomes and create a positive and productive learning environment. Embrace the power of teamwork and watch as your impact on students' lives grows exponentially.

As you can see, there are some important distinctions between groups and a team. The team is much more relationship-focused. Teams understand that they have influence beyond their classroom, that they aren't working in isolation, and that everyone works together. The highest performing schools have teachers who understand that these are all our kids (not just "the ones I teach"), and that we are in this together. When it is the "I" mentality and not the "team" mentality, teachers don't see faculty meetings as important, they don't see giving input for decisions to be necessary, and they may feel like they are competing against other teachers.

Cultivating Team Chemistry for Success

When a staff is team-focused, they have a unified vision and collaborate to help everyone be their best and bring their best! Functioning as a team is only part of it. Your team also needs chemistry to truly be effective. What is team chemistry? In a word, team chemistry is all about productivity. Teams with good chemistry are more productive because they understand what each member brings to the team and work to maximize strengths and minimize weaknesses of the other team members. Additionally, they manage their time better.

Teachers should have a great support system of peers/ colleagues/administrators. For example, when teachers receive negative specific feedback, they feel isolated. They are not sure who to go to or they may not want others to help because they're embarrassed. That's why it's important to have teams where they feel support and encouragement. It's also important for administrators to know teachers' needs and strengths, so they can provide support or have other teachers provide support. It's great when teams are high achieving, but the members of the team shouldn't be competitive or trying to undermine other team members.

Support builds morale within a team. You'll feel that your work is valued when you contribute to something that produces results. If you offer an idea that helps improve productivity, such as a new online communication system, confidence and trust is built within the team. Each team member has something unique to offer. By working together, members of a team feel a strong sense of belonging and deep commitment to each other and their common goals.

Team members want to work together for the good of the team and understand that combining the skills of numerous people will produce something that could not be created alone. The strengths of each team member are being utilized. As Babe Ruth once said, "The way a team plays as a whole determines its success. You may have the greatest bunch of individual stars in the world, but if they don't play together, the club won't be worth a dime." It is all about chemistry. Here are 6 strategies to creating team chemistry

1. Incorporate team activities
    Get your staff together and spend a day each month working on team-bonding. This is an important but

tricky one, because teachers already spend so much time at school and away from their families. Because of this, I would often use a PD day for these types of activities. There is no better way to get to know and appreciate your colleagues than to be around them and interact outside of the workplace setting. You may be thinking to yourself, "I'm around my colleagues 24/7, so why do I need to spend even more time with them?" Well, having a stronger connection with your fellow employees will make work more enjoyable and promotes a team mentality. Some examples of team activities include dinner, coffee, or maybe even an activity like bowling.

2. Create team goals and a mission statement
   It is important to establish common goals for your team. Create a day at the beginning of the year to sit down with your employees and establish these goals. When you do, split them up into teams of 4–5. First, set some "wish goals." These goals will be ones that are not likely, but you wish that you could accomplish them. Second, set goals that are reachable and realistic, but will be difficult to grasp. Last, set goals that you know for sure that you will accomplish as a team, ones that are fairly easy. Now, keep all these goals somewhere safe or post them to remind everyone of what they're working for. At the end of the year, you can evaluate how well your team has done. The next step is writing a mission statement. Like the first task, each group will come up with their own mission statement and then read them aloud. Then, combine each mission statement to create one that everyone agrees on. Remember to keep it short and concise.

3. Distribute tasks and responsibility evenly
   Everyone must work together and contribute in order to be successful as a company. Therefore, distribute certain tasks and divide responsibility among your staff based upon their strengths. It is important to allow employees, no matter their position, to be able to voice their opinions, give input and even lead certain tasks. Allowing each

member to feel vital to the team is essential in improving the school culture. Distributing the workload will also make it easier for each team member. Therefore, the work will be done more quickly and efficiently.

4. Build trust

    Trust is the most important variable of teamwork. If you do not trust your staff, then they will not be successful. In order to build trust, communicate with your staff and be open to their opinions. If a conflict arises, make sure you help to create a solution. Last, don't forget the Golden Rule. If you treat others the way you want to be treated, you will get the same in return. Building trust is the foundation of teamwork and is crucial to the success of the school.

5. Collaborate

    In education, we need to do a better job of collaborating. We have a false belief that if we seek help, we are incapable or not qualified. Everyone should seek mentoring and/or advice, from the superintendent to the novice teacher. This isn't weakness; this is seeking to be our best! We are not an island. One reason for burnout is isolation. Teachers speak an Affirmation language, so they need support and encouragement from their team. If we don't value collaboration, then we revert back to working in isolation where teachers tend to compete with each other rather than collaborating.

6. Make Others Feel Safe in Speaking Up

    Many times leaders intimidate their staff with their title and power when they walk into a room. Successful leaders deflect attention away from themselves and encourage others to voice their opinions. They are experts at making others feel safe in speaking up and confidently sharing their perspectives and points of view. They use their executive presence to create an approachable environment.

Empowering your staff to do the work that means the most to them, that they're best at, leads to building a truly dedicated team, and in the kind of stubborn, complex work we do, that means everything. Different people do their best work in different ways; we have extroverts and introverts among us, people with different strengths and specialties. It's important to trust the people you hire to do the job you hired them to do, give them the room and tools to grow and contribute but also stay close in touch. It's a kind of elastic dynamic that works when you attract and develop the right talent.

Team Synergy: the Power of We!

In the realm of teamwork, you'll find that the adage holds true: "A great team is greater than the sum of its parts." When you and your fellow educators come together, combining your unique strengths, skills, and perspectives, you create a collective force that transcends your individual capabilities. We call this phenomenon the power of "synergy," which means that the whole team becomes exponentially more powerful than the mere sum of its individual members. Geese in flight are often regarded as the pinnacle of "Synergy." This remarkable formation not only showcases the efficiency and coordination of geese but also holds valuable lessons for teams in various settings, including schools. We like to call this the power of "We"!

We even see this concept in team sports. Some of the greatest teams in history won consistently because they had a synergy. These teams may have had one or two superstars, but they won consistently because of their role players. The coaches knew how to maximize the strengths of the average players. These role players are the average players who perform consistently on a daily basis. They aren't superstars, but they are good and dependable. The coaches knew that when they put the right people in the right roles and gave them the tools necessary to do their job, success was all but guaranteed. So, it's not about having a school full of superstars; it's about maximizing the potential of the faculty you have. An important note here is that even your introverted teachers still have strengths and abilities, so the key is to place them where their strengths can be utilized. This makes it less about personality and more about what they bring to the team, which makes them more comfortable and perform better. Remember, even the greatest superstar needs teammates to make a great team.

As an administrator, you may have one or two superstars on your team, and if you're lucky, maybe even three or four, but you don't have a team full of them. So, build a great team by getting the best out of every teacher – not just the superstar, but everyone. Take the time to place teachers in the best position for them to succeed. This will ensure that your teams are working together as a cohesive unit.

You should have a clear vision or purpose. Remember the geese have a shared vision. It is not just some motto; they have a destination, and they all have to be on board with it to be successful. It's not enough to say, "We're the sixth-grade team of teachers." A purpose for being a team might be: "We come together as a team to support each other, learn from each other, and identify ways we can better meet the needs of our sixth-grade students." The purpose should be relevant, meaningful, and clear. It should not be just to hold more meetings or to check off some box about serving on a committee. Here are some key traits of a clear mission, based on the book "The Five Dysfunctions of a Team" (Lencioni, 2002):

- ◆ There are clearly defined, transparent goals aligned with the mission of the district.
- ◆ All team members are committed to these goals and to a clearly articulated plan of action.
- ◆ Goals are specific, measurable, attainable, realistic, and timely (SMART).
- ◆ There is shared clarity about how the work of the team will affect student achievement.

Team members don't have to be best friends, but they do have to build a level of trust to be effective. There needs to be trust in leadership, in teammates, and even in the established process. Teachers could grow complacent or frustrated if they don't feel their strengths are being utilized or their voices are being heard. Even when there is conflict, which is all but inevitable, it should be managed. There needs to be agreement about how we treat each other and engage with each other. There also needs to be someone, such as a facilitator, who ensures that this is a safe space. Furthermore, for there to be trust within a strong team, we see equitable participation among members and shared decision-making. Respect is an important part of trust because we value what each person brings to the team.

When we think of teams, horizontal ones (such as grade-level teams) usually come to mind. These teams are important because they help teachers focus on the best teaching and learning practices. Vertical teams are not as common in most schools, but they are visible in high-performing schools. They require a little more work to create but can be well worth it. The key is to ensure group members bring the right skills to the table and understand their job function. Underperforming teams often don't have the right skills they need to get the job done.

> Make sure your vertical teams have individuals with varying strengths to bring balance, such as an analytical person, creative person, etc. The teams that know how to work together and divvy up project tasks gain the most from their group's unique mix of knowledge and abilities. You may have some vertical teams in place, such as a leadership or curriculum team, but there are many potential teams that could help you create a high-performing school. According to an article in *The Balance* by Susan Heathfield (2016), five vertical teams are important to most organizations:
>
> ♦ The leadership team, which can include all administrators as well as department heads and others that you feel bring strengths to the team. The leadership team is the group that strategically leads your school.
> ♦ The motivation or morale team plans and carries out events and activities that build a positive spirit among employees. The team's responsibilities can include activities such as hosting lunches, planning picnics, fundraising for ill employees, etc.

◆ The safety or environmental team takes the lead in safety training, monthly safety talks, and the auditing of housekeeping, safety, and workplace organization. Recycling or even "going green" environmental policy recommendations are provided by the team as well.

◆ The culture or communication team works to define and create the defined company culture necessary for the success of your organization. The team also fosters two-way communication in your organization to ensure employee input up the chain of command. The team may sponsor the monthly newsletter, a weekly company update, quarterly employee satisfaction surveys, and an employee suggestion process.

◆ The teacher wellness team focuses on health and fitness for employees. Most popular activities include walking clubs, running teams, and periodic testing of health issues such as high blood pressure screenings. This team could set up events, such as a walking challenge to encourage the faculty to get moving more. Each participant could be given a pedometer to be downloaded daily at work. At the end of the challenge, there could be prizes for top performers.

By implementing these strategies and fostering a culture of teamwork, you can transform your school into a cohesive and high-performing institution. Encourage your teachers to shine and your school to stand out by making synergy of the team a priority. With a "We" approach, you will see increased unity, efficiency, and effectiveness among your staff.

Sharpen Your Winning Edge

1. Escape Room Challenge: Organize an escape room challenge where teachers work together in teams to solve puzzles, find clues, and escape within a given time limit. This activity promotes teamwork, problem-solving, and

effective communication while fostering a sense of shared accomplishment.

2. Collaborative Community Service Project: Plan a community service project where teachers come together to work on a meaningful cause outside of the school. This could involve volunteering at a local shelter, organizing a charity event, or participating in an environmental cleanup. Engaging in community service as a team helps build camaraderie, empathy, and a shared sense of purpose.

3. Goal Alignment and Collective Vision: Prompt teachers to reflect on their shared goals and collective vision as a team. Encourage them to consider: Are our individual goals aligned with the team's goals and vision? How can we ensure that our actions and decisions align with our shared purpose? What steps can we take to continuously reaffirm and reinforce our collective vision and goals as a team? How can we support and hold each other accountable for achieving these goals?

2

Principle 2: The Power of the V Formation

Have you ever seen a group of geese gathered near a pond or any other body of water? Their behavior can be particularly lively and loud. Geese are highly social animals, and when they congregate in these settings, their interactions and vocalizations can be quite energetic. In fact, a group of geese on the ground is called a gaggle.

Geese near a pond may engage in various activities such as feeding, grooming, or simply socializing with each other. During these times, their honking calls can reverberate across the area, creating a boisterous atmosphere. This is especially true when geese feel excited, threatened, or when they are communicating important information to the group.

It is not uncommon to witness geese splashing in the water, flapping their wings, and chasing each other, adding to the live-liness of the scene. These behaviors are natural expressions of their social dynamics and play an important role in their group cohesion and communication.

However, when geese are in the air, they are no longer called a gaggle, but are known as a team. And in flight, these teams fly in a V formation! The V formation serves as a remarkable represen-tation of what it truly means to be a team. As these majestic birds soar through the sky, their synchronized movement and unwavering unity exemplify the essence of collaboration, com-munication, and collective effort. Just like the geese, a team

DOI: 10.4324/9781003453819-3

embodies a shared purpose, cooperation, mutual support, and the recognition that together, they can achieve far more than what would be possible individually. The V formation not only showcases the remarkable capabilities of these avian creatures but also serves as an inspiring reminder of the power and effectiveness that lie within a truly cohesive team.

Soaring Together: Unlocking the Full Potential of Team

The V formation is not merely a coincidence but a deliberate strategy that maximizes the efficiency and effectiveness of the flock. Each goose positions itself slightly to the side of and behind the bird in front, taking advantage of the aerodynamic benefits. By doing so, they reduce air resistance and create a smooth flow of air, enabling the entire flock to fly with greater speed and consume less energy. In this way, the collective effort of the team becomes far greater than the sum of its individual parts.

Beyond aerodynamics, the V formation also serves as a masterclass in communication and coordination. Geese maintain visual contact with one another, allowing them to synchronize their movements and navigate with precision. The lead goose sets the direction, and the others follow, adjusting their positions accordingly. This seamless coordination ensures that the flock stays on course, even during long migratory journeys when accurate navigation is vital for their survival.

Moreover, the V formation fosters a sense of unity and mutual support among geese. As they fly in close proximity, they communicate through honking and vocalizations, reinforcing the bonds within the team. This communication serves multiple purposes, from signaling direction changes to offering encouragement and alerting the flock to potential dangers. By staying together and maintaining group cohesion, geese amplify their safety and response capabilities as they collectively detect predators or obstacles more easily.

In the context of education, this concept takes on profound significance. You and your colleagues, with your diverse backgrounds, expertise, and teaching styles, possess a wealth of knowledge and abilities. When you collaborate and work as a team, pooling your resources and talents, you amplify your impact on student learning and development.

Each member's strengths compensate for the weaknesses of others, creating a harmonious balance. One teacher might excel in instructional design and technology integration, while another may have a deep understanding of differentiated instruction and student assessment. By combining your strengths and collaborating on lesson planning, you can create dynamic, engaging, and effective learning experiences that cater to the diverse needs of your students.

Your team also thrives on collective problem-solving and decision-making. When faced with challenges or complex issues, each team member brings their varied perspectives and expertise to the table, resulting in more comprehensive and creative solutions. The power generated through collaborative problem-solving often leads to breakthroughs and innovative approaches that would have been difficult to achieve individually.

Teaching is a demanding profession, filled with ups and downs. In times of difficulty or stress, the strength of your supportive team becomes apparent. You can rely on one another for encouragement, guidance, and a sense of shared purpose, ultimately contributing to your individual well-being and job satisfaction.

Your team is far more than a collection of individuals working in proximity. It is a collective entity that leverages the unique strengths and perspectives of its members, fosters collaboration and communication, promotes innovative problem-solving, and provides emotional support. By embracing the power of teamwork, you can unlock your full potential and create remarkable outcomes for your students, surpassing what could have been achieved individually. So, continue to embrace the strength of your team and soar to new heights in your educational journey!

Applying the V Formation for Team Building

When you are building a team, you can gain valuable insights from the V formation of geese. By examining the key aspects of this formation, you can uncover principles that are applicable to team building in various contexts.

First and foremost, it is crucial to establish a clear structure within your team, just like the geese in the V formation. Designate a leader who can provide direction and guidance, while ensuring effective communication and interaction among team members. This structure promotes collaboration and efficient use of resources, allowing the optimal utilization of individual skills and talents.

Energy conservation is another important aspect of the V formation that can be applied to team building. In your team, you should foster an environment where team members can conserve their energy by distributing the workload and supporting one another. Effective task delegation, sharing responsibilities equitably, and leveraging individual strengths and expertise contribute to the team's efficiency while minimizing burnout (Lissaman & Shollenberger, 1970).

Efficiency is a key principle demonstrated by the V formation. To build the best team, optimize efficiency by assigning tasks and roles based on individual strengths and expertise. This ensures that each team member contributes in ways that lead to the highest productivity. Embrace a collaborative mindset where team members support and complement each other, facilitating more efficient and effective goal achievement.

Navigation and coordination are essential elements of the V formation, and they are equally important in team building. Geese maintain visual contact in their formation to navigate and coordinate their movements effectively. Likewise, establish clear lines of communication and coordination within your team. Encourage open and transparent communication channels, allowing the exchange of ideas, feedback, and progress updates. Regular team meetings, check-ins, and effective project management tools can help align the team's efforts toward a shared goal.

Flying in a V formation also provides safety and protection for geese, as they can collectively detect predators or obstacles more easily. Similarly, creating a safe and supportive environment is crucial in building the best team. Encourage a culture of trust, respect, and psychological safety within the team, where individuals can freely express their ideas, take calculated risks, and collaborate without fear of judgment or negative consequences.

Communication and social bonding are fundamental aspects of the V formation that can be applied to team building as well. Geese communicate through honking, promoting social bonding and maintaining group cohesion. Foster strong communication and social bonds within your team. Encourage active listening, constructive feedback, and open dialogue to build mutual understanding and trust. Team-building activities, shared experiences, and celebrating successes further strengthen social bonds and foster a sense of camaraderie.

Additionally, embrace a culture of learning and mentorship within your team, similar to how younger geese learn from the more experienced ones. Provide opportunities for knowledge sharing, mentorship programs, and collaborative learning experiences. This promotes a positive learning environment within the team, where individuals can acquire new skills, knowledge, and perspectives.

By understanding and applying the principles of the V formation to team building, you can create a cohesive and high-performing team. Establish a clear structure, conserve energy, maximize efficiency, promote effective communication and coordination, ensure safety and protection, foster social bonding, and embrace a culture of learning and mentorship. By embracing these principles, your team can navigate challenges, achieve their goals, and thrive collectively.

When educators work together in the right formation and going the right direction, the efficiency becomes palpable. You can see cohesion happening through lessons and also in planning while working together for the common goal of success in the tasks they are immersed with at that time. Supportive teachers talk about bad lessons, difficult student behaviors, unresponsive parents, and all other negatives in the profession. But they also talk about the positives!

They share their successes and why their lessons were awesome! They share strategies that worked and celebrate each other when the student or parent shows progress. From all of these discussions and communication, clarity can emerge, and efficiency takes over. They use the success to usher in more success and the daunting task of educating kids turns into the opportunity to make a difference. In a way, they begin to fly in a V formation, honking at each other as a way to help and assist as they achieve their goal.

It is important to point out that every time geese fly, they have that formation; however, they create the formation that works best for them. Sometimes there is an extra goose on one side, or perhaps one slightly not in line. It isn't because they don't want to be perfect, but because that is what works best for them at that time. The head goose trusts the geese behind her or him. The next two trust the geese behind them, and so on. The gaggle is a team, and they all play a crucial role in the formation.

Flawless Team Execution

Flawless execution is not about attaining perfection, but rather about meticulously preparing and executing the best game plan possible. It occurs when every team member is fully engaged, working harmoniously together, and supporting one another. Great teams inherently possess the qualities of a successful unit, but periodic reminders of essential practices are crucial to sustaining their success. In this chapter, we will explore key elements that teams should keep in mind to achieve flawless execution.

1. Collaboratively Create a Game Plan: To lay a solid foundation for flawless execution, it is imperative to involve every team member in the process of establishing goals and objectives. By inviting their input, the team ensures that everyone understands and aligns with the purpose and vision. People tend to be more invested in achieving goals they have helped shape. Therefore, fostering a collective sense of ownership and commitment is

essential. When creating the game plan, utilize the SMART goal framework (Rubin, 2002) to ensure clarity and effectiveness:

♦ Specific: Goals should be clear, concise, and easily understandable, avoiding ambiguity.

♦ Measurable: Define metrics or indicators that allow progress to be tracked and evaluated.

♦ Achievable: Goals should be realistic and attainable given available resources and constraints.

♦ Relevant: Goals should align with the team's overall purpose and contribute to its success.

♦ Time-bound: Set deadlines or timeframes to create a sense of urgency and accountability.

Example: Just as geese migrating together share a common destination, teams can collaboratively establish clear goals, such as aligning curriculum or test improvement benchmark.

2. Foster Effective Communication: Flawless execution heavily relies on effective communication. Geese, with their synchronized flight formations and constant honking, exemplify the importance of communication in team success. Similarly, teams must establish clear channels of communication and promote open dialogue. Regularly share updates, progress, and challenges to maintain alignment and ensure that everyone is well-informed. Effective communication fosters transparency, minimizes misunderstandings, and enhances collaboration.

Example: Geese honk to communicate during flight, guiding each other and maintaining formation. Teams can employ various communication tools, such as regular meetings, digital collaboration platforms, and active listening techniques, to ensure effective information exchange.

3. Clarify Roles and Cultivate Trust: Geese flying in a V formation exhibit the significance of role clarity and trust. Each goose has a specific role, and their synchronized movements demonstrate mutual reliance and trust.

In human teams, clarifying roles and fostering trust is equally vital. Clearly define each team member's responsibilities and ensure that everyone understands how their contributions impact the team's overall success. Nurture a culture of trust, where team members feel confident in each other's abilities and can rely on one another for support.

Example: Geese trust their fellow flock members to fulfill their roles within the formation. Likewise, teams can encourage trust-building activities, promote open feedback, and create an environment where individuals feel comfortable relying on their teammates.

4. Remember the Power of "We" Mindset: Teams can achieve flawless execution by fostering a culture of "We." Encourage team members to work together, leverage each other's strengths, and support one another. By combining their individual efforts, teams can achieve greater efficiency and overcome challenges effectively.

Example: Geese collaborate to reduce individual fatigue and maximize flying efficiency. Teams can facilitate collaboration through team-building activities, cross-functional projects, and creating an inclusive environment that values diverse perspectives.

Flawless execution is the outcome of a well-prepared game plan, effective communication, role clarity, and collaborative efforts. By involving every team member in goal setting, fostering effective communication, clarifying roles, and cultivating trust, teams can achieve remarkable outcomes. Like geese working in harmony during migration, teams that embrace these principles can execute flawlessly and achieve their shared objectives. Remember, flawless execution is not about pursuing perfection, but rather about the relentless pursuit of excellence through collective teamwork and support.

By functioning as a cohesive team, school staff can create an optimal learning environment for students, share resources and expertise, provide support to one another, and serve as role models for teamwork. The power of cohesive teams in schools should not be underestimated, as they have the potential to transform the culture, enhance teacher satisfaction, and improve student outcomes. Building and nurturing cohesive teams should be a priority for administrators, as it leads to remarkable achievements and success within the school community.

 ## Sharpen Your Winning Edge

1. Team Navigation Simulation: Organize a team-building exercise where team members simulate navigation in an outdoor setting. Assign different roles within the team, such as navigator, scout, and communicator. Encourage them to practice clear communication, visual contact, and coordination to reach specific destinations or complete challenges successfully.

2. Energy Conservation Challenge: Divide the team into pairs or small groups and assign them specific tasks or projects. Encourage team members to support each other, delegate tasks effectively, and find ways to conserve energy by leveraging each other's strengths and expertise. The goal is to achieve optimal efficiency and productivity while minimizing individual fatigue.

3. 360-degree Feedback: Implement a mechanism that allows you to gather input from teachers, enabling you to gain a comprehensive perspective on your leadership and teamwork. This valuable feedback can be collected through anonymous surveys or structured interviews, ensuring the honesty and openness of responses.

3

Principle 3: Effective Communication: The Key to Collaboration and Success

There needs to be a sense of urgency in education. At this moment, educators everywhere are pouring their hearts into lessons that will not get maximum results because they do not have clearly defined paths. Other educators are teaching standards that are not appropriate for the kids they teach, not because they are bad, but because they do not know any better. To be fair, some are still breaking out the dinosaur or penguin unit that they have dusted off for the past 28 years of their career. The reason these examples and others are happening is because of a lack of clear communication.

Geese flying know how to get the most out of their day, and teachers should learn to do the same. They know how to get the most out of each other, and teachers should be relentlessly moving students forward. Principals should be challenging staff to be better daily and giving them the opportunity to succeed in the position where they can be the most successful, whether that is a grade-level chair, assistant principal, committee leader, etc. Yet, because they are often unwilling to have courageous conversations, or even talk at all, inefficiency is everywhere.

DOI: 10.4324/9781003453819-4

Communication is key for geese, as it enables them to coordinate their movements and maintain formation. Through honking and vocalizations, geese communicate important information to the rest of the flock, such as signaling direction changes or adjustments in flight path. This coordination ensures that the entire flock stays aligned and moves together, maximizing their collective efficiency and navigation.

In terms of navigation, communication plays a crucial role. By maintaining visual contact and continuously communicating with each other, geese can stay on course and reach their destination. Communication helps geese make real-time adjustments to their flight path, allowing them to respond to environmental cues such as wind patterns or landmarks. The ability to communicate and make collective decisions on the best route to follow enhances their navigation capabilities.

Communication also serves as a warning system for the safety of the flock. Geese can alert the rest of the flock to potential dangers, such as predators or obstacles, through vocalizations. This early warning system enables the entire flock to respond quickly and adapt their flight behavior to avoid threats. The collective awareness facilitated by communication increases the overall safety and protection of the flock.

Furthermore, communication strengthens the social bonds and group cohesion among geese. By constantly honking and vocalizing during flight, geese reinforce their sense of togetherness and unity. This social bonding is essential for the flock's well-being and survival, as it fosters cooperation, mutual support, and a shared purpose. Effective communication helps maintain group cohesion, ensuring that the flock remains together and benefits from the collective advantages of flying in a V formation.

Additionally, communication allows geese to synchronize their movements and actions. Honking and vocalizations help geese maintain a consistent pace and rhythm within the formation. This synchronization enhances the overall efficiency of flight and minimizes disruptions or disarray within the flock. By communicating and synchronizing their actions, geese can optimize their collective performance and conserve energy during long flights.

Overall, communication among geese flying in a V formation plays a critical role in coordination, navigation, warning
and safety, group cohesion, and synchronization. These communication advantages enable geese to maximize their collective
efficiency, adapt to changing conditions, and enhance their
chances of successful migration. The principles of communication observed in geese flying can serve as valuable lessons for
effective communication within teams, promoting collaboration,
coordination, and shared goals.

Probably most importantly, geese use communication to provide support and encouragement to their fellow flock members.
Honking serves as a motivational tool, helping geese stay
connected and offering reassurance during challenging flight
conditions. When one goose is struggling or fatigued, the others
will honk and show support, encouraging it.

The Importance of Open Communication

In order to cultivate a strong sense of teamwork among teachers,
effective communication and collaboration are essential. Open
lines of communication and regular channels for exchanging
information and aligning instructional practices create a foundation for successful collaboration. By establishing these communication channels, teachers can share insights, stay updated on
important developments, and ensure that everyone is working
toward common goals.

A culture of continuous learning further enhances teamwork among teachers. By encouraging effective communication
as a catalyst for growth, schools can inspire teachers to share
their expertise, experiences, and resources with one another.
This sharing of knowledge enables teachers to navigate the ever-
evolving educational landscape more effectively. Opportunities
for communication and collaboration on curriculum development, instructional strategies, and assessment practices allow
teachers to adapt and respond collectively to changes in education.

Creating a supportive environment is also crucial for effective
teamwork. When teachers feel comfortable sharing challenges or

obstacles they face in their classrooms, it promotes collaboration and problem-solving. Schools can establish platforms for professional discussions, mentoring programs, or peer observations to foster continuous improvement and ensure the well-being of both students and teachers.

In addition, strengthening social bonds and group cohesion plays a vital role in building effective teamwork. By promoting effective communication, schools can encourage collaborative practices such as co-planning, co-teaching, or participation in professional learning communities. These activities provide opportunities for teachers to actively communicate, share insights, and support one another. Recognizing and celebrating teachers' achievements, organizing team-building activities, and cultivating a positive and inclusive school culture foster a sense of unity and shared purpose among the teaching staff.

Facilitating synchronization in instructional practices is crucial for creating a consistent and coherent educational experience for students. Effective communication plays a vital role in ensuring that teachers share best practices, strategies, and resources. By encouraging the sharing of these valuable assets, schools can promote a collaborative approach to instruction. Additionally, fostering a culture of reflection and feedback allows teachers to provide constructive input and engage in professional dialogue, leading to enhanced collective performance.

Open communication and collaboration are foundational elements in cultivating a strong sense of teamwork among teachers. By establishing open lines of communication and regular channels for information exchange, teachers can share insights, stay informed, and work toward common goals.

Overcoming Challenges and Embracing Effective Strategies

"We gotta talk." This was perhaps the most important line spoken by Harry (played by Robert Duvall) in the movie *Days of Thunder*. The film about a race-car driver and his crew, who overcome many professional and personal obstacles, takes a turn with those four tiny words. Up until that point, the racing team had not won, or even finished the race due to all kinds of failure. Their body language showed great despair, as there were fights, tantrums, sarcasm, and negative passive-aggressive actions. Even when Harry walks up to the driver, he finds a person slumped at a bar with a look of anger, sorrow, and defeat. However, once Cole (Tom Cruise) and Harry have that difficult conversation, the momentum begins to build and outcomes change. That little statement led to them starting to communicate effectively and learning what each person needed to hear so that they could become more efficient in their practice. You see them begin to trust each other, listen intensively with better body language, and positive change occurs at a fast pace.

When we confront problems and conflict from a viewpoint of working to fix the issue, we start with clear communication. Educators are no different than racing crews when it comes to teamwork. Each person has a definite role to play, and the goal is to become as flawless as possible, whether it be at changing tires during a pit stop or teaching reading or math.

Once educators work together in the right formation and going the right direction, the efficiency becomes palpable. You can see cohesion happening through lessons and in planning while working together for the common goal of success in the tasks they are immersed in at that time. Supportive teachers talk about bad lessons, difficult student behaviors, unresponsive parents, and all other negatives in the profession. But they also talk about the positives! They share their successes and why their lessons were awesome! They share strategies that worked and celebrate each other when the students or parents show progress. From all of these discussions and communication, clarity can emerge, and efficiency takes over. They use the success to usher in more success and the daunting task of educating kids turns into the opportunity to make a difference. In a way, they begin to fly in a V formation, honking at each other as a way to help and assist as they achieve their goal.

It is important to point out that while every time geese fly, they have that formation, they do create the formation that works best for them. Sometimes there is an extra goose on one side, or perhaps one slightly not in line. It isn't because they don't want to be perfect, but because that is what works best for them at that time. The head goose trusts the geese behind her or him. The next two trust the geese behind them, and so on. The gaggle is a team, and they all play a crucial role in the formation.

In any organization, effective communication is the cornerstone of success. This holds true for schools, where the exchange of information among administrators, teachers, and support staff plays a crucial role in fostering a productive learning environment. However, common communication comes with challenges. Here are four examples of how information is disseminated in a building.

1. **Top down, trickle approach.** Most times, a principal and admin teams talk to grade-level or department chairs. The "chairs" are tasked with leading the conversations and passing along information to their teams. The teams may then be expected to pass items along to support staff members. That is a lot of channels for pertinent information to travel through in a consistent manner. The chance of all crucial information getting to the ears of the right people is slim.

2. **Telephone game.** A person is told to tell a colleague something. The colleague tells it to another person and so on. By the time it gets to everyone, the correct message is lost.

3. **The middle-man (or -woman).** A person tells someone to let a group of people know relevant items, but then skews it their way depending on their perspective. The people who hear the perspective then take it how they heard it, put their personal bias into it, and the true message is now lost.

4. **The questioner.** In a whole-staff meeting, the agenda is set and as soon as the first item comes up, that one teacher or staff member wants to ask multiple clarifying questions. This leads down a rabbit hole, causing many others to check out. Body language drops to the negative, and before you know it, the time is up, and the main message was lost or not communicated effectively.

So how do we change this when there are so many meetings and so many things happening in a school? That is the ultimate challenge. Here are two suggestions.

1. **Have fewer meetings.** More meetings equal more opportunities for misconceptions and poor details. There is no reason to have a meeting just to have a meeting. Not everyone in the school needs to hear everything. Do not waste the time of people to whom the relevant information is not relevant. People need to be focused on certain tasks and be efficient in those tasks. Inefficient communication takes away from the efficiency of the teams. They can maximize their time in other ways.

2. **One meeting via a digital forum.** Recording any pertinent information that needs to be said can be sent out online in a video. Attach an agenda and people can then listen to just the information they know pertains to them. If they have any thoughts or clarifying questions, schedule a time for them to get all the extra info they need. This forum also allows playback in case somebody missed what was stated, or if there turns out to be any confusion about certain aspects of the meeting. In the end, if the leader of a school says what needs to be said clearly, and nobody can then implement the telephone game, you have eliminated all four issues described earlier.

Whether it be the geese reaching their destination or educators of all kinds receiving positive data, praise, or uplifting feedback in some way, the statement "communication is key" remains true. Without it, exhaustion and failure often will occur. Races are not won with the driver alone, and if the geese don't work together, burnout will happen, which results in them not traveling as far as they should have that day. Educators know that feeling all too well, and many want to make a change in a positive way. To start this process, someone needs to be willing to say, "We gotta talk."

 ## Sharpen Your Winning Edge

1. Conduct a group activity where each team member selects an educational topic they are unfamiliar with but willing to learn about and share with the group. Allow

other team members to write down these topics and identify who is willing to offer assistance by saying "We gotta talk" to support their fellow colleagues.

2. Ask all staff members which of the four ways stated they feel is the most common communication forum on campus. Then complete a discussion regarding that type of communication in order to address it with the purpose of fixing the problem or enhancing the output.

3. Nonverbal Communication Analysis: Reflect on your nonverbal communication cues, such as body language, facial expressions, and tone of voice, during team interactions. Consider how these nonverbal cues can influence the effectiveness of your communication. Identify ways to improve your nonverbal communication to ensure alignment between your intended message and how it is perceived.

4

Principle 4: Maximizing Team Success by Harnessing Individual Strengths

Norman Dale, head coach of the basketball team from the small town of Hickory, Indiana shows us how applying the "V" principles to his role in the movie *Hoosiers* will lead to ultimate success. He comes into his new position knowing that he is following a successful predecessor who passed away suddenly, a community that doesn't much like change, and he is fighting his own demons at the same time. Yet through his clear communication with various people in his life, we see him transform a team by knowing the importance of recognizing individual strengths and assigning roles accordingly. Along the way, not only does the group of young men he is leading gain confidence in him, as does the town and his harshest critic, but he gains a belief in their leadership and abilities as well. They all learn to support each other even when they disagree vehemently. Then at the end, we see it all come to a moment where three little words change everything as one of his basketball players, Jimmy, says, "I'll make it."

Each school district has clearly defined roles and each role has clearly (usually) defined responsibilities. From the superintendent, through the principal, down to the support staff, into

DOI: 10.4324/9781003453819-5

the community, back around to the voters who elect the school board, which gets us back to the superintendent, this structure can be somewhat compared to geese as they fly in their formation.

After all, the V formation of geese involves several roles that contribute to the team's success. The lead goose sets the direction and pace, navigates through different conditions, communicates with the team, and motivates them. The wing geese provide support, coordination, and stability on either side of the lead goose. Follower geese maintain the formation, benefit from reduced air resistance, and cooperate with the team. Rotating geese share leadership responsibilities, maintain energy levels, and ensure efficiency. The backstop goose watches for stragglers, ensures safety, provides support, and maintains the integrity of the formation. These roles demonstrate the importance of coordination, balance, and teamwork in achieving goals.

When geese begin the day's flight, there is very clearly a leader who points them in the right direction as they take off and the rest are expected to follow. All the other geese joyfully get in line where they belong and where they can do their best work, helping the team as they move toward their destination. They honk with joy as they make their way, happy to help as the success of the team is paramount. Yet, along the way, something happens that is built into their DNA.

The Importance of Knowing Each Team Member's Strengths

As a school leader, having a deep understanding of the strengths and talents of your staff members is essential for effective leadership and the overall success of your school. Knowing the strengths of your staff allows you to strategically allocate resources, build cohesive teams, and provide targeted support and professional development opportunities. By recognizing and leveraging the individual strengths of your staff, you can foster a positive and productive work environment, enhance job satisfaction, and ultimately improve student outcomes. This section explores why it is important for principals to know the strengths of their staff and how this knowledge can positively impact the school community.

Building a team based on individual strengths requires a strategic approach that leverages their unique abilities and talents. You can employ the following key strategies to build a team focused on individual strengths:

◆ Assess Your Team Members' Strengths: Start by conducting assessments or surveys to identify the strengths, skills, and talents of each team member. Encourage them to engage in self-reflection and self-assessment to gain insights into their own capabilities. Utilize tools such as strengths-based assessments or personality assessments to gather comprehensive information about individual strengths.

◆ Align Roles with Strengths: Once you have identified individual strengths, align roles and responsibilities based on those strengths. Assign tasks and projects that capitalize on each team member's abilities, enabling them to excel and contribute meaningfully. This alignment ensures a more efficient and effective team, as individuals are working in areas where they naturally thrive.

◆ Encourage Collaboration and Skill Sharing: Promote a collaborative environment where team members can share their strengths and expertise with one another. Encourage cross-functional collaboration, allowing team members to learn from each other and develop a broader range of skills. Create opportunities for skill sharing sessions or workshops where individuals can showcase their strengths and provide guidance to others.

◆ Foster a Strengths-Based Culture: Cultivate a culture that values and celebrates individual strengths. Encourage your team members to embrace their strengths and recognize the unique contributions they bring to the team. Regularly acknowledge and highlight individual strengths and successes, fostering a positive and supportive team environment. By appreciating and leveraging strengths, your team members will feel valued and motivated to excel.

By implementing these strategies, you can build a team that maximizes individual strengths, leading to increased productivity, satisfaction, and overall team success. Remember, each team member has unique talents to offer, and by recognizing and utilizing those strengths, you create a cohesive and high-performing team.

Hire for Strengths, Manage for Success

I have often said that we hire teachers for their strengths, yet we manage them based on their weaknesses. The irony of most hiring is that we seek out candidates who will bring value to the position. We look for people with a strong resume and talents that stand out. However, once we have this perfect candidate in place, the focus becomes more about improving performance or fixing weaknesses than it is about improving the strengths on which they were hired. I remember my first year of teaching in a very large school system. I was looking forward to bringing my talents and strengths to my new job. However, within the first few weeks of school, I was given something called a PAC, which was a personal appraisal cycle that was meant for me to focus on areas of improvement for the school year. So, I was basically required to spend my first year of teaching focusing on two or three areas that I felt needed improvement. This is not a unique situation when you consider that most employees are evaluated with a performance review, which usually focuses on areas of growth, which is just a nice way to say "weaknesses." What strengths does your staff bring? If we think of the staff as a team, then we need people with different talents and skills.

For instance, if we were creating a sports team, everyone can't be the quarterback or the running back, and not everyone can be a receiver. The key to success is to put people in positions where they can be most effective. Then look for other opportunities for them to grow even more, specifically if they are seeking out new opportunities.

It is important for you to hire and focus on the strengths of teachers because doing so can have a significant positive impact on the overall school environment and student outcomes. Here are a few reasons this approach is crucial:

♦ Enhancing job satisfaction: When teachers are recognized and valued for their strengths, they feel a sense of fulfillment and satisfaction in their work. Focusing on their strengths allows them to excel in areas where they have expertise and passion, leading to increased motivation and engagement.

♦ Building a collaborative culture: By hiring teachers based on their strengths, principals can create a diverse team of educators with complementary skills and talents. This fosters a collaborative culture where teachers can learn from one another, share best practices, and work together to address challenges. Collaboration and teamwork among teachers contribute to a supportive and enriching learning environment for students.

♦ Maximizing instructional effectiveness: Teachers who are given the opportunity to focus on their strengths are more likely to excel in their instructional practices. By aligning their strengths with the needs of the students and curriculum, principals can optimize the learning experience for students. When teachers are able to leverage their strengths, they can deliver high-quality instruction that meets the diverse needs of their students.

♦ Promoting professional growth: Focusing on the strengths of teachers allows principals to provide targeted professional development opportunities that align with individual teacher needs. By investing in their strengths, principals can help teachers further develop their expertise, which not only benefits the individual teacher but also contributes to the collective growth of the teaching staff.

♦ Retaining talented teachers: We definitely have an attrition problem in this country. There is a near-50% turnover every 5 years. When teachers feel valued and supported in their areas of strength, they are more likely to stay in their positions and contribute to the long-term success of the school. By recognizing and nurturing their strengths, principals can create a positive work environment that promotes teacher retention, reducing turnover and ensuring stability in the school community.

◆ Finally, we need to hire for strengths, and we need to manage for strengths. This means that we don't just evaluate teachers, but we treat them as professionals who are looking to maximize their strengths and potential. I suggest instead of the traditional evaluation or end-of-year evaluation that you include aspirational conversations. These conversations help you understand the goals and needs of each staff member to really help them be the best teammate possible.

There are six key questions to ask staff on a regular basis, in place of the event, such as an employee review (a review ultimately focused on what they need to work on, or a focused set of questions regarding employee improvement). In education, this suggests formative assessment (ongoing, interim) in place of summative assessment (the test, the autopsy to determine if one passed or failed). These six questions become more productive.

Aspirational Conversation
1) Have we helped you succeed?
2) What do you think we do well? Such as reading, extra-curricular, etc.
3) What do you see, such as in other schools, that would make us do better?
4) What would make you want to leave us?
5) How can I best support you right now?
6) What are your professional goals? How can we help you achieve them?

People often leave because they're not valued and because there is no room to grow. Does one desire to work toward an administrative role? Or maybe take on a different role in the school? Tell them you will help them get there. Value them by letting them know that if they will be the best teacher they can be every day for you, then you will help them achieve their goals

Nurturing Teacher Engagement: Empowering Educators for School Success

As a school leader, it is crucial to ensure that teachers do not feel overwhelmed by these additional roles but instead see them as opportunities to contribute to the school's success. Here are some key points to emphasize:

- ◆ It is crucial to emphasize the value of their expertise and encourage them to share it with others. By participating in mentorship programs, teachers can provide guidance and support to new or less-experienced teachers, helping them navigate the challenges of teaching and acclimate to the school culture. This collaborative sharing of knowledge can strengthen the entire teaching community and contribute to the school's success.
- ◆ Highlight the personalized support available: Instructional coaches can work closely with teachers on an individual basis to enhance their teaching practices. Assure teachers that these coaches are there to provide one-on-one support, observe classroom instruction, and offer constructive feedback tailored to their specific needs and goals.
- ◆ Recognize the impact on curriculum and instruction: Teachers involved in curriculum development play a crucial role in ensuring that the curriculum aligns with educational standards, is engaging and relevant, and promotes coherence across grade levels or subjects. Emphasize that their efforts contribute to the overall quality of education provided by the school.
- ◆ Communicate the benefits of professional development: Professional development facilitators can organize targeted training sessions and workshops to enhance teachers' instructional practices. Emphasize that these opportunities are designed to support their growth and provide ongoing support to help them improve their teaching skills.
- ◆ Explain the importance of data-informed decisions: Data analysts can collaborate with teachers to analyze student

assessment data and provide insights to inform instructional decisions. Emphasize that working with data analysts can help teachers develop data-driven strategies, interventions, and support systems that lead to improved student outcomes.

◆ Promote collaboration and leadership: Encourage teachers to take on leadership roles such as team leaders, PLC leaders, or committee members. Highlight the benefits of facilitating collaborative team meetings, coordinating planning efforts, and fostering effective communication among team members.

◆ Foster family and community engagement: Highlight the role of parent communication coordinators and community engagement coordinators in building positive relationships with parents and involving the local community in the school's activities. Emphasize the importance of bridging the gap between the school and the broader community to create a supportive and enriching environment for students.

◆ Support well-being and morale: Stress the significance of wellness advocates, morale boosters, and health and wellness committee members in promoting teacher well-being and fostering a positive work environment. Recognize their efforts in organizing wellness initiatives, recognition programs, and activities that enhance job satisfaction and teamwork.

But by emphasizing the value and benefits of these additional roles, teachers are more likely to embrace them as opportunities for personal and professional growth, rather than feeling overwhelmed by added responsibilities. Encourage open communication and provide necessary support to ensure a successful integration of these roles within the school community.

Essential Roles Teachers Play in Fostering School Team Success, Wellness, and Morale

In the dynamic world of education, a diverse range of roles exists to support the growth and development of educators and students alike. These roles encompass facilitators, consultants, designers, coordinators, and advocates, each playing a crucial part in fostering an enriching and inclusive learning environment. Let's explore some of these key roles and their significance:

The key here is to find teachers who are passionate about these areas or feel like they have strengths in these areas. Otherwise, it may just feel like you are trying to add more to their plate. And truthfully, it is better if some of these roles go unfilled if teachers aren't excited about partaking in them.

Facilitator: As mentors, educators provide guidance and support to new or less-experienced teachers. They share their knowledge and expertise, offer advice, and help navigate the challenges of teaching. Mentors play a crucial role in helping new teachers adapt to the school environment, providing instructional support, and fostering professional growth.

Teaching Consultant: Teaching consultants collaborate closely with colleagues to improve their teaching practices and instructional strategies. They offer personalized support, observe classroom instruction, and provide constructive feedback to empower teachers in enhancing their instructional effectiveness. Teaching consultants work alongside educators to develop customized plans for professional growth.

Educational Content Designer: Educators involved in curriculum development collaborate with their peers to design and create educational materials and resources. They ensure the curriculum aligns with educational standards, create engaging and relevant lessons, and ensure coherence across different grade levels and subjects. Educational content designers continuously review and update curriculum materials based on the evolving needs of students and educational research.

Technology Integrator: Technology integrators assist colleagues in effectively integrating technology into their teaching practices. They stay updated on the latest educational technologies, provide training and support, and help teachers incorporate technology tools and resources into their instruction. Technology integrators promote digital literacy and help teachers use technology to enhance learning outcomes.

Inclusive Education Collaborator: Inclusive education collaborators work with special education professionals to support students with diverse learning needs. They collaborate on developing individualized education plans (IEPs), provide instructional strategies and accommodations, and ensure inclusive practices in the classroom. Inclusive education collaborators promote collaboration and effective inclusion of students with special needs.

Professional Growth Facilitator: Professionals specializing in facilitating professional development activities lead workshops, training sessions, and communities of practice to enhance the professional growth of teachers. They identify areas that require development, organize and deliver targeted training, and provide ongoing support to help educators improve their instructional practices.

Collaborative Leader: Collaborative leaders facilitate team meetings, coordinate planning efforts, and foster effective communication among team members. They actively contribute to goal setting, distribute responsibilities, and ensure that the team's work aligns with the school's vision and objectives. Collaborative leaders provide invaluable support, guidance, and feedback to promote collaboration and maximize productivity.

Community Engagement Coordinator: Community engagement coordinators initiate partnerships and organize events to involve the local community in the school's activities. They collaborate with community organizations, businesses, and individuals to create opportunities for students, such as inviting guest speakers, organizing career exploration programs, or coordinating community service projects. Community engagement coordinators help bridge the gap between the school and the broader community.

Assessment Coordinator: Assessment coordinators oversee the implementation and coordination of various assessments in the school. They ensure assessments align with educational standards, provide training on assessment administration, and coordinate the collection, analysis, and reporting of assessment data. Assessment coordinators help maintain the integrity and effectiveness of the assessment process.

Well-being Advocate: Well-being advocates promote and support teacher well-being by organizing wellness initiatives and activities. They raise awareness about self-care, stress management, and work-life balance. Well-being advocates may organize workshops, wellness challenges, or provide resources to support the physical, mental, and emotional health of teachers.

Diversity and Inclusion Advocate: Diversity and inclusion advocates promote diversity, equity, and inclusion within the school community. They raise awareness about cultural competence, support inclusive practices, and advocate for equitable opportunities for all students. Diversity and inclusion advocates work collaboratively with teachers, students, and families to create an inclusive and welcoming environment.

Positive Behavior Support Coordinator: Positive behavior support coordinators implement strategies and programs to foster positive student behavior and create a supportive school climate. They collaborate with teachers, staff, and administrators to develop and implement behavior support plans, provide training on positive behavior management, and promote positive reinforcement strategies.

By embracing and valuing the contributions of these diverse roles, educational institutions can create a holistic and nurturing environment that promotes student growth, supports teacher development, and ultimately enables every individual to thrive. Through collaborative efforts, these roles combine to form a cohesive and comprehensive educational system dedicated to empowering students and educators alike.

Defining Responsibilities to Succeed

To lay the foundation for a cohesive and accomplished team of educators, it is paramount to first grasp the purpose that unites them. This understanding must align with the overarching mission and objectives of the educational institution or school. By clarifying the team's purpose, educators can gain a deeper comprehension of how their individual roles contribute to the overall success of the team and the students they serve.

Promoting collaboration is equally vital as responsibilities are delineated. Educators must recognize the interconnected nature of their roles and understand that collaboration is a key factor in ensuring student achievement. Nurturing a culture of teamwork involves fostering regular meetings, encouraging the sharing of best practices, and promoting support and learning among colleagues. Collaboration facilitates the exchange of ideas, the development of innovative approaches, and collective problem-solving, all of which are essential for overcoming challenges.

Establishing accountability is of utmost importance in ensuring that responsibilities are fulfilled effectively. Expectations for each role should be clearly defined, encompassing specific goals, deadlines, and quality standards. Regular monitoring of progress, along with providing feedback and recognition for achievements, is crucial. Open communication and collaboration among team members create an environment where challenges and concerns can be addressed proactively.

Once the key obligations have been identified, the next step involves assigning specific roles to each team member. This process should be collaborative, taking into account each educator's expertise, experience, and individual strengths. By aligning responsibilities with educators' interests and strengths, their motivation and job satisfaction can be enhanced.

Effective communication plays a vital role in ensuring that responsibilities are understood by the entire team. Providing written documentation that outlines each educator's roles and responsibilities, along with relevant resources and guidelines, is essential. Meetings and workshops should be conducted to ensure clarity and comprehension of individual and collective responsibilities. Encouraging open dialogue and addressing questions and concerns fosters ongoing alignment and reinforces the importance of each team member's contribution.

By defining responsibilities within a teacher team, a solid foundation is established for a successful and high-performing educational unit. Through a shared purpose, the identification of key obligations, role assignments, accountability, collaboration, and effective communication, educators can seamlessly work together and maximize their collective impact on student learning. Clear responsibilities provide the necessary guidance, structure, and sense of purpose to empower the team to confidently tackle the challenges of education and achieve their shared objectives.

Sharpen Your Winning Edge

1. Have every team member pick two colleagues and write down their perception of the area in which they are a leader, then challenge those who were chosen to lead PD in those areas so that capacity is built within the group.

2. Have staff write down an area of their job they are comfortable in, and one they are not comfortable in. Have them share and challenge other staff members to use their strengths to help others where they struggle.

3. Reflective Journaling: Encourage teachers to keep a reflective journal where they can document their experiences, challenges, and successes in their additional roles. Prompt them to write about their feelings, insights, and lessons learned. This activity allows teachers to process their thoughts and emotions, gain clarity, and identify areas for growth.

5

Principle 5: Navigating the Storm: How Educators Adapt to Learning Challenges

Many "V" principles can be taken from the movie *Apollo 13* and adapted to life, as well as the educational profession. There are clear examples of each of them throughout the movie. As soon as Tom Hanks (as Jim Lovell) uses very clear communication and says, "Houston, we have a problem," the entire team must adapt immediately to the situations that begin to come at them. One of the biggest hurdles was finding a way to get the crew home. When finding out that they do not have enough power to make it to Earth, the leader of the mission (Gene Kranz, played by Ed Harris) says, "Gentlemen, that's unacceptable!" Then, following more discussion, he emphatically says the statement that he is known for: "Failure is not an option."

The *Apollo 13* movie, and real life at that time in 1970, covered every "V" principle in many ways. We are shown clear communication between the crew on Earth and in the spaceship. There are defined roles and responsibilities with ample collaboration (and inner competition for one astronaut back in Houston as he fights exhaustion and obstacles to find the procedure needed to get the power on). The astronauts encourage and support each other, even after they have some tense words at times, as they

DOI: 10.4324/9781003453819-6

trust and rely on the engineers working on each problem. There is diversity of thought and inclusion of all people who may help find answers. Roles of leadership or followership emerge, many times showing people playing both roles at some point in the film. In the end, the astronauts reach Earth safely and you hear Tom Hanks saying that NASA coined their mission "The Successful Failure," because they didn't land on the moon but were successful in getting back home.

In our profession, the COVID-19 pandemic was our "successful failure." Failure in the fact that we did not have the opportunity to educate kids in a "normal" way, but successful in the fact that we educated kids well, given the circumstances surrounding us. We were "geese" in so many ways.

Distance learning was a perfect storm for so many educators. If you remember, the world seemingly shut down in March of 2020, and schools were still largely tasked with finding a way to educate their students after classes were canceled. Walking out of the classroom one day and not being able to return any time soon, yet still being told to find a way to teach kids, was a monumental challenge. Throw in the idea that we were inundated with bad news across the world daily, facing fear from every direction, and yet this crazy expectation to keep kids learning somehow was a ridiculous ask given to the educators in that moment. People in our profession care about kids, so many felt it was their duty to assure kids and provide some time of respite for them away from the chaos, all while worrying about their own families and friends. It was literally a pandemic in many ways, and one that the best storyteller could not have written. Yet, like geese, educators found their way and rose from the ashes to educate students in the best way possible, always adapting to the latest regulations like wind patterns, navigating other storms, and, perhaps most importantly, taking care of each other.

Here are some ways in which the school teams adapted during the pandemic:

1. Emphasis on Remote Learning: COVID-19 necessitated a rapid shift to remote learning as schools faced closures

and the need to maintain educational continuity. Schools had to quickly adapt their instructional methods to online platforms, utilizing digital tools and resources to facilitate virtual learning experiences. Remote learning became a central focus, requiring teachers to develop new skills in delivering effective online instruction and engaging students remotely.

2. Technology Integration: The pandemic accelerated the integration of technology in education. Schools had to invest in digital infrastructure, provide devices and internet access to students, and train teachers in using online learning platforms and tools effectively. The increased reliance on technology transformed how schools deliver instruction, facilitate communication, and assess student progress.

3. Hybrid Learning Models: Many schools adopted hybrid learning models that combined in-person and remote instruction. This hybrid approach allowed smaller class sizes, social distancing, and reduced risk of COVID-19 transmission. Teachers had to adapt their lesson plans, instructional strategies, and assessment methods to accommodate both in-person and remote learners, creating equitable learning experiences for all students.

4. Focus on Health and Safety: COVID-19 led to a heightened emphasis on health and safety protocols in schools. Teachers had to adapt their classrooms, implement social distancing measures, enforce mask-wearing, and enhance cleaning and sanitization practices. Adapting to these new protocols required teachers to establish routines and procedures that ensured a safe learning environment while minimizing disruptions to instruction.

5. Increased Collaboration and Support: The pandemic highlighted the importance of collaboration and support among educators. Teachers had to come together as teams to share best practices, collaborate on lesson planning, and provide emotional support. Virtual staff meetings, professional development webinars, and online collaboration platforms became essential tools for teacher collaboration and support.

As educators, we have the internal fortitude to fly like geese and utilize the "V" principles, and we proved it during the pandemic. So why are we not continuing to follow them now whenever we have a chance?

In the "We gotta talk" scene mentioned in Chapter 3, we see a very resistant driver not willing to talk to the crew chief. He wants Harry to set up the car so that it fits his style, which Harry is willing to do, but Cole won't tell him what he needs in order to drive the car and win. When Harry asks him why he won't tell him, the race car driver has to admit that it is "because he doesn't know much about cars." A huge admission for someone that is supposed to win races! However, the lack of success they are having drives him to swallow his pride and make that statement. You see him at his most vulnerable, taking the risk to put a little bit of trust in the person he met a few months ago. This led to him beginning to learn about cars, which shows his adaptability, much like geese who are in mid-flight.

Like Cole, teachers have to admit when they do not know something. Support staff, administrators, central office, parents, everyone must be willing to be vulnerable for the sake of change. One of the most powerful, commonly used, and dangerous phrases in education is "we've always done it that way." If educators are not willing to adapt to the times and changes set forth by the world, we are not preparing students to be ready for the life ahead of them. The goose at the head of the formation must let the others know when he or she is tired so that the team can replace him or her. When the person in front is a true leader, they admit they cannot lead and move to a spot where they can still be part of the team and let others more powerful take the lead.

Weathering the Storm

As mentioned earlier, COVID-19 and the pandemic changed teaching forever. There was no choice but to adapt. Failure was not an option in 2020, just as it wasn't in 1970. Adjustments had to be made, and without those changes to distance learning, kids would have been lost to a higher degree than they potentially were. Collaboration was paramount the first few days after summer in July and August as everyone scrambled to learn online programs and build new digital classrooms using their Bitmojis. And a miraculous thing happened. The majority of educators **adapted** to meet the circumstances and were flexible with their methods. They talked about programs, resources, digital lessons, and grew exponentially through their willingness to adapt and change.

In the eyes of educators, COVID-19 was essentially the equivalent to a severe thunderstorm, or maybe even a tornado, for the geese in flight. It changed the entire course of education and set us back. But like the geese who hit turbulence, educators must change and meet the challenges together. They need to be willing to be open and honest and say that they don't know much about a resource or program, a strategy, how to handle that difficult parent, or perhaps even teaching in general. This would be almost the same as a race-car driver admitting they don't know about cars.

Geese have to be flexible as they adapt to the weather minute by minute, day by day. They adapt to more or fewer geese in their formation, or to any potential health issues a goose may face. Regardless they help, each using the tools and instincts they have, again being flexible with their methods. If they did not adapt, their chance of survival decreases rapidly.

Another scene that relates to this flexibility and the ability to adapt within the movie *Apollo 13* occurs when they have to find a way to make a carbon dioxide filter using just the items they know the astronauts have on the ship that can be spared. An actor pours a bunch of materials out on a table and says, "We have to make this [a round cartridge] fit into this [a square filter] using nothing but that. Let's get it organized." In the end they find a way, having been flexible with their knowledge of what each piece of material can do and adapting to their circumstances. They made their V formation in that room and worked through the problem.

When the pandemic hit, teachers essentially had to find a way to make a square peg fit into a round hole, just like the group in *Apollo 13*. They were given a bunch of items and found a way to make it work, becoming flexible in their methods and adapting on the fly.

When it comes to adapting to these storms, the three most important keys for teams are:

1. Effective Communication: During challenging times, maintaining open and effective communication within the teacher team is crucial. Clear and timely communication helps to share important updates, coordinate efforts, and address any emerging issues. By staying connected, team members can provide support, exchange ideas, and ensure that everyone is on the same page, enabling a coordinated response to weather storms.

2. Embracing Innovative Approaches: To effectively embrace change, teacher teams must be open to exploring and implementing innovative approaches to teaching and learning. This could involve experimenting with new technologies, instructional methods, or educational resources. By embracing innovation, teacher teams can better cater to the diverse learning styles and needs of their students, creating a dynamic and engaging classroom environment.

3. Collaborative Problem-Solving: The ability of teacher teams to come together and engage in collaborative problem-solving is vital during storms. By pooling their collective knowledge, skills, and experiences, team members can brainstorm creative solutions, address challenges, and develop strategies to support student learning in adverse conditions. Collaborative problem-solving fosters a sense of shared responsibility and empowers the team to find effective solutions that benefit all students.

Education as we knew it died in 2020. However, out of this storm, many fantastic adaptations occurred. Computer programs became better at adapting to kids and meeting the needs of teachers. Educators found that some of the changes were for the better, and they upgraded.

However, in 2023 we are, in many ways, longing to get back to when we were all working together to solve issues. We need to focus on the "V" principles now more than ever, because, as Gene Kranz perfectly pointed out nearly 50 years ago, "Failure is not an option." If geese fail, they die, and while educators do not have stakes quite that high, if they fail, kids suffer, and the ripple effect is immeasurable moving forward.

A Closer Look at Adaptability Traits for Successful Teams

Education is constantly evolving, and teacher teams play a vital role in shaping the learning experiences of students. To thrive in this dynamic environment, these teams must embody certain key qualities that contribute to their success. So, let's take a look at the essential qualities that make teacher teams effective and impactful.

Effective teams cultivate an approach that welcomes new ideas, perspectives, and approaches. They embrace change and remain receptive to innovative strategies that address the evolving needs of education. By fostering a mindset of exploration, they can discover effective methods that enhance learning outcomes and create engaging classroom experiences.

Strong teams possess excellent problem-solving abilities. They analyze challenges, think critically, and collaboratively develop creative solutions to overcome obstacles. By working together and leveraging their collective expertise, they find effective ways to address complex issues that arise in the classroom. This problem-solving mindset ensures that students receive the support they need to thrive academically and personally.

When faced with unexpected situations or setbacks, resilient teachers exhibit the ability to bounce back. They maintain a positive attitude and adapt their plans to meet the needs of their students and the team. They persevere in the face of adversity, finding innovative ways to navigate obstacles, and remain committed to providing a high-quality education experience.

Collaboration lies at the heart of successful teams. They prioritize teamwork and cooperation, creating an environment that values collective efforts. By actively working together, leveraging each other's strengths, and sharing ideas and resources, teacher teams enhance their collective impact. This collaborative spirit ensures that students receive comprehensive support and benefit from diverse perspectives.

Finally, they embrace the value of lifelong learning. They expand their knowledge, stay updated with best practices, and engage in professional development opportunities. By continuously refining their skills and staying informed about the latest advancements in teaching methodologies, they enhance their effectiveness as educators.

When teacher teams embody these qualities and work together, they create a positive and dynamic learning environment. Students benefit from the synergistic efforts of educators who are open-minded, skilled problem solvers, resilient in the face of challenges, collaborative in their approach, and committed to continuous learning. With this strong foundation, teacher teams empower students to reach their full potential and foster a lifelong love for learning.

Flexibility Traits for Successful Teams

The ability to be flexible and adaptable are highly desirable traits for a team. Teams that embrace flexibility as a core value are better equipped to navigate the ever-changing landscape of education and provide students with a dynamic and enriching learning experience. In this section, we delve into five vital aspects of flexibility in teaching and explore how they contribute to the success of teacher teams. From openness to change and creativity to time management, versatility, and adaptability to students, we will unravel the significance of these qualities and their profound impact on creating a nurturing and responsive educational environment.

Flexibility starts with being open to change. Teachers who are receptive to new ideas, methodologies, and approaches foster an environment of innovation and growth. By embracing change, these teachers are constantly seeking ways to improve their practice and staying up to date with the latest research and pedagogical advancements. Their willingness to adjust plans, strategies, and approaches ensures that they are meeting the evolving needs of their students and providing them with the best possible education.

It's also important to possess a creative mindset that allows them to think outside the box and find alternative solutions to challenges. They understand that no two students are alike, and they actively seek innovative approaches to meet the diverse needs of their learners. By leveraging their creativity, these teachers can tailor their lessons and instructional methods to engage students and promote deep learning. They encourage curiosity, experimentation, and critical thinking, fostering a classroom environment that nurtures creativity and encourages students to explore their own unique perspectives.

Flexible teams work collaboratively, valuing teamwork and cooperation. They actively engage in open communication, sharing ideas, insights, and resources. By leveraging the collective expertise of team members, they find innovative solutions and foster a supportive environment.

Flexible teams demonstrate adaptability by adjusting to unexpected situations or challenges. They remain calm and composed, quickly modifying their plans to address the needs of students and the team. They are willing to step outside of their comfort zones and explore different approaches to achieve desired outcomes.

They also possess strong problem-solving abilities. They analyze challenges, think critically, and develop creative solutions collectively. By approaching obstacles with a solution-oriented mindset, they overcome barriers and ensure the smooth functioning of the team and the success of their students.

Flexibility is the cornerstone of effective teaching and learning. By embracing openness to change, nurturing creativity, mastering time management, cultivating versatility, and adapting to individual student needs, teacher teams can create a nurturing and responsive educational environment. Let us celebrate and embrace the power of flexibility in education, as it holds the key to unlocking the full potential of both teachers and students.

Lead Goose in the Storm

During a storm, the lead goose assumes a critical role in guiding and protecting the flock. It determines the flight path, faces the wind resistance, and creates a slipstream for the geese behind. Acting as a visual reference, it helps the flock maintain formation and avoid disorientation. Adapting to the conditions, the lead goose alters strategies and provides support to boost morale. Through its leadership, resilience, and adaptability, the lead goose leads the flock through adversity to safety.

As you can see, one of the most important traits of a leader is to be visible and accessible during a storm or crisis, much like during the COVID pandemic. It is during crisis that your team may depend on you the most! You should be creating a climate of trust, collaboration, and teamwork by adding encouragement, support, and praise. Rising to the occasion during tough times is not an easy task, but it is critical to creating a positive working environment. As a leader, make sure things are better and not worse, or as I like to say: add to the calm, not to the chaos.

Let me take you back to an extraordinary experience I had a couple of years ago while flying to Malaysia. I was en route to speak at teaching centers across the country, and we had already been in the air for about ten hours, soaring along the coast of Russia toward Japan. Little did I know that an unexpected storm was lurking ahead. Suddenly, turbulence struck with a vengeance. It was the dead of night, and although most passengers were fast asleep, I remained wide awake. You see, I have trouble sleeping on airplanes. I have this irrational sense that I need to be alert, as if the pilots might call upon me for assistance in navigating the aircraft.

As the plane shook violently, jolting us with bumps and drops, the pilot's voice crackled over the speaker. His instructions were clear and urgent – flight attendants were to take their seats and fasten their seatbelts immediately. The panic was palpable among the flight attendants as they hastily secured themselves. Yet, amidst this turmoil, something fascinating occurred: the pilot's voice remained steady, devoid of fear. He spoke to us with unwavering calmness as our aircraft was tossed like a salad, 30,000 feet above the ground.

For what felt like an eternity but was likely only a brief period of ten minutes, the pilot skillfully guided us through the tempest. In those intense moments, I couldn't help but entertain the possibility that it might be our final journey. However, when the plane finally found stability, and the passengers erupted into cheers of relief, I approached a flight attendant with a request. I asked her to convey our heartfelt appreciation to the pilot for his remarkable composure under such extreme pressure. He had created an atmosphere of tranquility amidst what could have easily become a chaotic and panic-stricken situation.

This gripping incident serves as a powerful reminder that in times of crisis, we all have the potential to be the pilot – the steady hand guiding others through the storm. Whether you are the pilot of a plane, the thermostat of a school, or any analogy that resonates with you, remember that during tumultuous times, all eyes turn to you. Take a deep breath, center your focus on the issues at hand, and make decisions that contribute to a sense of calm rather than chaos.

You possess the ability to set the tone, to influence the environment around you. You can be the steady force that instills confidence, trust, and resilience in others. So, embrace this role, and lead with unwavering determination. When faced with adversity, be the pilot who steers their crew and passengers to safety. Be the thermostat that regulates and maintains a climate of stability and optimism. Your actions and choices can have a profound impact on those around you.

Let your presence in a crisis be a beacon of hope and a source of inspiration. Take charge, for you are the one everyone looks up to when the storm clouds gather. Remember, in the face of uncertainty, it is your calmness, your ability to focus, and your wise decisions that will guide others through the turbulence.

Sharpen Your Winning Edge

1. Have each teacher highlight an area of change they have made after the pandemic and share it with a colleague in order to provide both leadership and collegiality.

2. Challenge each staff member to name a time when they felt like they failed, yet persevered and grew because of it. Share what adaptations they made to resolve the issue.
3. Make a diagram of all the ways teachers are flexible through the day, week, month, and year. Take the results and highlight the most frequent, and then discuss ways to avoid any common pitfalls in those areas.

6

Principle 6: The Power of Collaboration: Fostering Team Unity

When the Vegas Golden Knights reached the Stanley Cup finals in their inaugural year, thousands of hockey fans packed the arena to witness what would have been one of the most improbable stories in sports. The idea that a team in their first season could win the final series in hockey was inconceivable to many.

As the team became more and more beloved in Las Vegas, the community saw teamwork that was second to none. The team was known as "The Golden Misfits," because they were essentially a group of players that were no longer wanted by their former teams. Strangers came together to work toward a common goal, and while they ultimately came up short in the end, they proved that the sum of the parts is greater than just one person. In many ways, they were geese, working together toward that common goal. Geese can often play for other teams, join different groups as they make their way to the end of the journey, yet they never compete with each other. The competition was a burning desire inside of each player to do better for their team, which made each player improve, and that resulted in better collaboration and teamwork. They only work together to make their way to their destination. The "Golden Misfits" came

DOI: 10.4324/9781003453819-7

together, created their own V formation, took care of each other, and headed in the same direction, doing their part along the way.

When it comes to collaboration versus competition, educators, for some reason, tend to be more competitors than collaborators. They take on the role of an "independent contractor." Many stay in their rooms, often not sharing ideas, doing their own thing. Many hope to not talk to people unless necessary or forced to in a mandated PLC session. Further, many do not buy into data, or even look at the numbers when it comes to the success of their students. Many also scoff at the teachers who go above and beyond, who engage kids, who do fun activities, and who are beloved by administration, students, and parents. But why is that?

In almost all other professions, if you take the approach of an "independent contractor," you rarely have success. Teamwork is mandatory in many professions. Surgeons work with nurses, lawyers rely on clerks, construction workers rely on each other in their various roles, and they know that one is just as important as the other when it comes to reaching a goal. In the school arena, without specialists or support staff, as well as special education teachers, the school simply will not run.

However, with the field of education being different, the "independent contractor" can do their thing as described here, and be relatively assured they will still be employed the next year. It is easy to blend in with the crowd in many schools because if the majority of students are having success, the school could be deemed successful, and why change what is working? Another scenario of mediocrity may be that the teacher works in a very affluent school, kids come in performing at grade level, parents work with them as needed, the teacher doesn't have any complaints, and the status quo continues to be status quo, which is ok for them.

When it comes to competition, the "independent contractor" doesn't really care how they perform because they do not have to. In their mind, they do their thing, and if it works, great. They are only responsible for the kids in their class and once they move onto the next grade, a new batch of students marches into their room to endure mediocrity.

Nearly every successful coach will tell you friendly competition is a good thing for the improvement of the players and the team as a whole. Playing against worthy opponents makes players better. Iron sharpens iron, as the adage says.

Every teacher should want to be as successful as they can, which translates into grade-level success. Every grade level should perform at a high level because it translates to school-wide success. All support staff should want to assist the licensed staff so that they make a difference in the outcomes of students. However, human nature causes people to measure themselves against those they feel are equals as a way to assess their ability. In a way, it requires competition, because each person should want to compete to be better. But who should you compete against?

The answer is simple. Each teacher needs to compete against themselves. They should strive to be better than they were the day, week, month, and year before. Each teacher should strive to grow in all areas and leverage their personal growth into student success. Following that competition from within, collaboration should follow, and that requires another word in the process: comparison.

In the National Football League, offensive linemen from all teams come together each off-season to share their expertise with each other in an effort to move their specific position forward. Defensive linemen heard about this and started their own off-season camp to keep up with the players they were routinely going up against in games. By working with each other and sharing the tricks of the trade, their colleagues could then use their new ability and skills to be more successful against their opponents, and success leads to more lucrative contracts. This is precisely how educators should think. They should collaborate through comparing techniques and abilities so they can compete internally to get better. It is the idea many take when they attend conferences. Presenters drive collaboration between participants who then internally compete with themselves to get better at their craft. Every competitor in these practices must reflect on their practice and make adjustments in order to get better, and this same strategy should apply to educators.

When teams "compare" their results and look at how each of them completed tasks, the collaboration leads to increased success for all of them. They share the same goal of overall improvement, which leads to the ability to communicate in all forms. Great teams collaborate in many ways that lead them to make gains in all areas. If you think about the "geese" described in the beginning, they "compare" their stamina and ability to the others and assist as needed based upon the outcomes.

The Golden Knights were a prime example of teamwork, as are most professional sports teams. Ronald Reagan said, "There is no limit to the amount of good you can do if you don't care who gets the credit." Nobody cared who scored the goals in that inaugural season; they only cared about the total goals the team scored. Nobody cared who blocked shots. The backup goalie didn't mind that he wasn't playing. The end goal was all about the team. The fact they made it to the Stanley Cup Finals cemented them in hockey lore. Even though the team's roster has changed in the past few years, the current team is still the model of success. The highest-paid player celebrates when the lowest-paid player scores. When someone starts a scrum, everyone on the ice goes to the defense of the player in the middle of it. It is a Three-Musketeer mentality of "All for one, one for all." This belief should be no different for other teams. In many cases, people just want to be a part of the success in whatever way possible. If educators can create teams that work in this same way, their success will never have a ceiling of possibilities. They need to create their own "V" formation to help with efficiency.

The Importance of Collaborating

Collaboration is the key to success in any organization, and schools are no exception. When teachers, administrators, and support staff work together as a cohesive team, the educational experience is greatly enhanced for both students and educators. The importance of teams collaborating within a school cannot be overstated, as it leads to improved outcomes, increased innovation, and a supportive environment for all.

First and foremost, collaboration among school teams leads to improved outcomes for students. When teachers collaborate, they can share best practices, discuss student progress, and identify strategies to address individual needs. This collaborative approach ensures that all students receive a high-quality education tailored to their unique requirements. For instance, a teacher might notice that a student is struggling with a particular concept and seek advice from a colleague who has successfully taught that topic before. By working together, teachers can develop effective interventions and support systems, ultimately leading to improved academic performance and increased student achievement.

In addition to academic success, collaboration fosters a culture of innovation within a school. When teams collaborate, they bring together diverse perspectives, expertise, and ideas. This diversity of thought fuels creativity and problem-solving, enabling educators to find new and inventive ways to engage students and enhance the learning experience. For example, a team of teachers may collaborate to develop interdisciplinary projects that integrate multiple subjects, fostering critical thinking and encouraging students to make connections across different disciplines. By leveraging the collective intelligence of the team, schools can create an environment that nurtures innovation and prepares students for the challenges of the future.

Furthermore, collaboration within a school creates a supportive environment for all stakeholders. Teachers who work in isolation may feel overwhelmed or isolated, especially when facing complex challenges. However, when teachers collaborate and support one another, they can share the workload, divide responsibilities, and provide emotional support. Collaborative teams can also serve as a source of professional development, where educators can learn from each other's experiences and build their skills. Administrators can play a crucial role in fostering this supportive environment by encouraging collaboration, providing resources, and recognizing and celebrating the achievements of teams. When educators feel supported and connected, they are more likely to be satisfied with their work and perform at their best, ultimately benefiting the entire school community.

It is important to note that collaboration within a school is not limited to teachers alone. Effective collaboration requires the involvement of all stakeholders, including administrators, support staff, parents, and students. When all members of the school community work together toward a common goal, the synergy created is truly transformative. For instance, administrators can collaborate with teachers to develop and implement schoolwide initiatives, parents can collaborate with teachers to support learning at home, and students can collaborate with their peers to deepen their understanding of the subject matter. Such collaboration fosters a sense of belonging, ownership, and shared responsibility, creating a positive school culture and climate.

In conclusion, collaboration within a school is of paramount importance. When teachers, administrators, support staff, parents, and students collaborate as a team, the educational experience is enriched, leading to improved outcomes, increased innovation, and a supportive environment for all. As we continue to navigate the complexities of education, fostering collaboration should be a priority, as it is through collective effort and shared expertise that we can truly unlock the full potential of our schools and empower our students to succeed.

Collaboration Over Competition

The support and appreciation you provide is crucial in shaping the culture among teachers. Without adequate support, team competition can be negative. Principals play a pivotal role in cultivating a positive environment that promotes collaboration and minimizes the negative effects of team competition, benefiting the entire school community. For instance, if you neglect to recognize and appreciate the efforts of your teachers, it can cause unnecessary competition. For example, when teachers feel undervalued or ignored, they may seek attention and validation from the principal as a way to gain recognition for their work. This behavior can arise from a desire for validation and a need for job satisfaction.

When teachers compete instead of collaborating, it can indeed create team dysfunction within a school. Competition, when taken to an extreme, can undermine teamwork, hinder progress, and negatively impact the overall educational environment. Here's a closer look at how teacher competition can lead to team dysfunction and why collaboration is a better approach:

> In this environment, teachers may be reluctant to share resources, strategies, or best practices with their colleagues. This withholding of information prevents the free flow of knowledge and hampers the collective growth of the team. Collaboration, on the other hand, encourages open communication and the sharing of ideas, ultimately benefiting all teachers and students.

When teachers are focused solely on outperforming their colleagues, it can create an atmosphere of isolation and limited support. Instead of seeking assistance or collaborating on problem-solving, teachers may view their colleagues as rivals, hindering the creation of a supportive and cohesive team. Collaboration promotes a sense of camaraderie and a willingness to work together, ensuring that everyone can benefit from collective expertise and support.

A competitive environment can elevate stress levels among teachers as they constantly strive to outdo one another. The pressure to perform better than their colleagues can lead to burnout and diminish job satisfaction. Collaboration, on the other hand, distributes the workload, encourages shared responsibility, and reduces individual stress levels. By working together, teachers can support each other and create a healthier work-life balance.

When teachers are in competition with each other, the focus can shift from student learning to personal success. Collaboration allows educators to pool their strengths, develop comprehensive teaching strategies, and ensure that students receive a well-rounded education. When teachers work together, they can create an environment where students thrive academically and socially.

To address team dysfunction caused by competition, it is crucial for school leaders to foster a culture of collaboration. This can be achieved through professional development programs that emphasize the value of teamwork, creating opportunities for teachers to collaborate on projects and initiatives, and recognizing and celebrating collective achievements. School leaders play a pivotal role in promoting collaboration and modeling the behavior they wish to see among the teaching staff.

So, while healthy competition can have some positive effects, an excessive focus on competition among teachers can lead to team dysfunction within a school. Collaboration, on the other hand, promotes a supportive, cooperative, and inclusive environment where teachers can collectively work toward achieving common goals. By prioritizing collaboration over competition, schools can foster teamwork, enhance professional growth, and create an environment that benefits both educators and students.

Building Team Unity

A cohesive team is more than just a group of individuals working together. It creates an atmosphere that fosters deep friendships and unwavering loyalty. Within this tightly knit web of relationships, employees are not only motivated to put in extra effort but also to actively collaborate and support one another. It's no secret that each team member possesses their own unique set of strengths, weaknesses, communication skills, and habits. However, when a teamwork environment is neglected or absent, it poses significant challenges to achieving the overarching goals and objectives. Instead of focusing on collective success, employees become fixated on promoting their individual achievements, which can hinder overall progress.

In the realm of education, one aspect often overlooked is the competition that arises among teachers when a true team concept is lacking. Teachers find themselves engaging in silent rivalries, vying for better-looking classrooms, superior lessons and units, and even greater approval from parents. This unhealthy competition stems from a profound sense of underappreciation they receive from their administration. When teachers feel unrecognized or undervalued, they inadvertently start competing with their peers for attention and acknowledgment. This detrimental cycle can only be broken by cultivating a team-oriented mindset, where teachers realize they are not in competition with one another, but that they are there to uplift and enhance each other's abilities. This newfound unity within the teaching community creates immeasurable value for all its members.

Yet building such unity is not always an easy task, as teaching has long been viewed as an isolated profession. Even the once-hallowed teachers' lounge has transformed into a mere pitstop for snacks or checking mailboxes, devoid of collaboration or relationship development. The relentless demands on teachers' time make it challenging for them to connect and reach out for support. Consequently, many teachers feel like they are battling their professional challenges alone, with nowhere to turn when things go awry. However, with cohesive teams in place, teachers can find solace in a robust support system comprising peers, colleagues, and administrators. For instance, when teachers receive specific negative feedback, they often experience isolation, unsure of whom to approach or reluctant to seek assistance due to embarrassment. This underscores the importance of fostering teams where teachers feel a genuine sense of support and encouragement. It is equally vital for administrators to understand the unique needs and strengths of their teachers, enabling them to provide targeted support or facilitate peer assistance. While achieving high levels of success is commendable, it is crucial that team members refrain from engaging in competitiveness or undermining one another. A harmonious team thrives on mutual support, with each member working collaboratively toward shared goals.

Support within a team serves as a cornerstone for building morale. When your contributions directly contribute to tangible results, you feel a deep sense of value and appreciation for your work. By presenting an idea that enhances productivity, such as implementing a new online communication system, you not only bolster confidence but also foster trust within the team. Each team member possesses a unique skill set and perspective, making their collaboration indispensable. Through their collective efforts, team members experience a profound sense of belonging and forge a profound commitment to one another and their common objectives. They recognize that by leveraging the diverse skills of numerous individuals, they can create something far greater than what any individual could accomplish alone. The strengths of each team member are not only recognized but actively utilized, ensuring the team's success becomes a shared triumph.

Effective Collaboration Strategies for Great Educational Teams

So how can great teams in education collaborate effectively? There are many ways that teachers can collaborate to enhance their teaching and benefit their students. Here are some examples of teachers collaborating:

1. Co-planning lessons: Two or more teachers can work together to plan a lesson or unit that integrates multiple subjects or perspectives.
2. Team teaching: Teachers can team up to co-teach a class or subject, bringing their unique expertise and teaching styles to benefit the students.
3. Sharing resources: Teachers can share lesson plans, materials, and resources with each other to save time and effort and ensure that all students receive high-quality instruction.
4. Peer observation and feedback: Teachers can observe each other's classes and provide constructive feedback to help improve their teaching practices.
5. Professional development: Teachers can attend workshops, conferences, and other professional development opportunities together to learn new teaching strategies and stay up to date with the latest research and trends in education.
6. Collaborative assessments: Teachers can work together to develop and administer assessments that measure student learning across multiple subjects or learning objectives.
   #1. Co-planning lessons: Two or more teachers can work together to plan a lesson or unit that integrates multiple subjects or perspectives. This is an easy place

to start because very few teachers enjoy planning lessons, much less planning every single lesson alone. Discussing the standard, the vocabulary, and ways to engage students, ending in assessment of learning, should be easy for educators to discuss. Once the first one is planned, the rest should become easier as teammates become more comfortable with each other.

#2. Team teaching: Teachers can team up to co-teach a class or subject, bringing their unique expertise and teaching styles to benefit the students. While this can be a difficult area, if two or more teachers have bought into the notion that they can work together well and be successful, it can be very beneficial to students. Taking this approach requires trust to initiate it, so working together when trust is already established should come easily.

#3. Sharing resources: Teachers can share lesson plans, materials, and resources with each other to save time and effort and ensure that all students receive high-quality instruction. As another very easy step, this is highly prominent via social media. Multiple teachers can share ideas via Instagram or TikTok that are then taken by other teachers who can utilize them in their classroom. Using a digital forum to share lesson planning, making materials for each other, and sharing videos or other ideas doesn't take much effort once a relationship is created in some way.

#4. Peer observation and feedback: Teachers can observe each other's classes and provide constructive feedback to help improve their teaching practices. Watching your peers is a powerful way to gain perspective on better ways to enhance the craft of teaching. Many times, just walking into another classroom can spark an idea or give someone a thought that can lead to better outcomes. Giving feedback on what you see while in someone else's classroom not only provides affirmation for the person being observed but also causes the observer to reflect on their own practice.

#5. Professional development: Teachers can attend workshops, conferences, and other professional development opportunities together to learn new teaching strategies and stay up to date with the latest research and trends in education. Watching other professionals who have knowledge of teaching can be powerful. If a presenter has current knowledge of the pedagogy and can relate to the participants, professional development will lead to positive results.

#6. Develop and administer collaborative assessments: Collaborate with other teachers to design and implement assessments that measure student learning across multiple subjects or learning objectives. By aligning assessment practices, teachers can ensure consistency and identify areas for improvement. Collaborative assessments also provide opportunities for data analysis and collaborative decision-making to enhance instructional practices.

Having a common goal of being the best in your field is essential. When people share a mission, students tend to grow at a rate of nearly 4 times the norm. Grade levels that can grow students at that rate are rare, but it can be done, and the way to accomplish this goal is through collaboration as mentioned in these steps.

 Sharpen Your Winning Edge

1. Self-reflection. What did I learn from collaborating with my colleagues? Did their perspectives and experiences provide new insights and ideas for my teaching practice? How can I integrate these learnings into my classroom?
2. Highlight monthly each of the seven forms of collaboration and focus on enhancing them school-wide through a variety of discussions and tasks.

3. Cross-Grade Level Collaboration: Organize joint projects or activities that involve teachers from different grade levels. This can include designing interdisciplinary units, sharing resources, or aligning curriculum to ensure a smooth transition for students as they move from one grade to another.

7

Principle 7: Investing in Team: The Power of Support and Motivation

COVID-19 was essentially a tornado to the geese flying south for the winter. It changed the entire course and set us behind. But like the geese who hit unexpected turbulence, educators must change and meet the challenges together. When geese see a storm approaching or run into a strong headwind, they adjust or find a way to wait out the hazards in front of them. Teachers had a strong headwind facing them when the pandemic hit, and they had to change. There was no choice but to adapt to the situation. Even today, they need to be willing to say that they don't know much about certain resources or programs, a strategy, how to handle that difficult parent, or perhaps even teaching, which is equal to a race-car driver saying they don't know about cars.

While an entirely different animal than a goose, in the book *If You're Riding a Horse and It Dies, Get Off*, author Jim Grant does a fabulous job of providing the opportunity to connect the idea of a horse dying to many problems that occur in life, and the text definitely applies to education as a whole. He also discusses ways to make the horse work again, which leads to an epiphany. You can break it down to many circumstances within the profession, which are discussed at the end of this chapter.

This book is a metaphor for many other areas in a larger broader sense of education. Sadly, many people in power feel like they need to push people even more when they are already breaking

DOI: 10.4324/9781003453819-8

down as a form of encouragement and support. However, some see it as the idea that "a bigger whip" or the thought that possibly yelling at the subordinates could help a dire situation. Sometimes a possible solution includes the suggestion of a new rider, meaning a new administrator for a school or perhaps a change in superintendent of the school board. The book's suggestion of "a new saddle, better food, or some motivation" covers teacher concepts such as recommending new programs, fancy materials, or that for kids, better nutrition will lead to better results. Superintendents and unions constantly want to throw money at the problem, and politicians believe a better assessment measure might be necessary, both of which are suggested in the text. Supervisors consistently form "committees" to look at areas of concern and gather input from stakeholders. Finally, just like someone in the book flat-out calls the horse lazy, this is symbolic of the public and various stakeholders who wish to blame educators and kids for the problems that the profession faces on a daily basis.

While the book includes parallels to the "V" principle of "encouragement and support" at times, it also does it in a way that is contrary to how the geese would approach the problem.

When flying, geese are seen supporting each other during long flights and challenging times. They consistently provide and receive constructive feedback from each other not only by doing their part in the "V," but their honking is positive and lets the others know that the team is there for them. The importance of encouraging and supporting team members to build morale and confidence can be seen as they make noise to encourage their gaggle and push each other to be better. During their journey, if one of their team members becomes ill or injured, another goose stays with that one until it is healed or passes away, doing what it can to help at any time and giving up its own personal goals for their teammate. This positivity and support leads to greater team cohesion and success, and educators are no different! In the end, relationships mean more than nearly anything else in a school. Without those, you cannot move the building forward at the rate that you should be. When people value and respect each other, they will always do more than is expected for their colleagues, which creates huge momentum in a school. To refer back to the horse and rider, even they can do so much more if they know and trust each other, and their relationship is in balance.

Rethinking Encouragement

When we examine other ways to approach "a dead horse" in education, let's do some "what ifs" in the form of positive support and encouragement.

What if, rather than using a louder voice, we spoke with encouraging words and let our actions be positive and helpful to those going through the problems they are facing at the time?

What if we use the same people, but provide constructive criticism and positive feedback to them so that they could improve their practice and build capacity, thus using their resources better instead of forcing them into using other resources that may not work as well as the previous ones?

What if we didn't spend good money on products that won't make a difference in the outcomes? How about we take the programs we have and replace only the parts that are broken and not the whole thing, so that some familiarity remains as we learn how to use the updated version?

What if we didn't try to fix issues with items that will not provide better results or have zero to limited return on investment of time? One example of this would be creating a new form that breaks down learning standards a different way but gets the same results. All too often, teachers hear they have to break down each standard so they know what is in it in order to teach it well. While that might be true, they do not need to fill out forms, or a different form, to prove they know what they are doing. Administrators need to look at the outcome and ask, what if there was a better use of time that made lessons more engaging? How about letting the professionals pick the supplies or resources they need to meet the needs of their room or students or personally?

What if we actually gave teachers things that motivate them in a positive way, rather than providing negative reinforcement through negative actions or behaviors? How about we actually get to know our people and assist them in a positive way and provide positive reinforcers that are differentiated based upon the likes or desires of each person in our system? As mentioned earlier, relationships matter more than almost anything when it comes to educating kids. What if we knew each staff member and what they valued? If you were to look at the love languages, some staff members would like a well-written card (words of affirmation), and some would like you to provide lunch or snacks (acts of service). If we know our staff, we can better use that knowledge to get the most out of them, leading to a better outcome overall.

What if, rather than throwing money at every problem, we put it all back into the people so that they flourish and don't leave the field of education? How about throwing the money you have at salaries or stipends to be spent on supplies (with accountability built in), so that professionals can do what they believe is right for their kids and be rewarded financially for their outcomes?

What if we only had one assessment, three times a year, which measured whether each teacher is growing all kids? If they are, we repeat all the positives from each "what if," and if they are not, we repeat each positive from every "what if" in that situation as well? What if we didn't base how successful educators were on assessments that don't focus on the right areas? What if we assessed schools on how well they are creating humans with a work ethic and a growth mindset, as well as how well they achieve success in academics?

What if we just got rid of all committees forever? How about if we need a group of professionals to discuss something relevant, we ask for volunteers? What if the volunteers were actually invested in the topic that was being discussed, rather than being forced into a committee when they really don't care or don't know anything about the topics covered in meetings?

What if educators were revered rather than thought of as "lazy"? 99.9% of educators are not lazy, and their efforts should be acknowledged and reinforced somehow by the public.

At the end of the book, a young kid says, "I know what to do! If you're riding a horse and it dies . . . get off and try something new!" What if we actually listened to kids? They often show us what they need, how they feel, or provide feedback on if our approach is helping them learn. What if every educator recognized that sometimes what they're doing might not be working, and when that happens, they must try something new? What if leaders completed all of these suggestions for the people around them?

In many ways, the profession has moved onward and upward after the pandemic, with many new approaches through technology as well as better resources that are relevant to all kids. However, in 2023 and going forward, the profession is also still riding the same dead horses from before the world shut down in March 2020. Many of our old ways will not get us anywhere. Geese never stay still; they always adjust to their circumstances, and if something isn't working, they move on, or encourage others with support. They have to – because in those moments, it is life or death. Educators, as individuals and as teams, should do the same because for some kids, the stakes are critical to their lives. After all, as Alexander Den Heijer states, "When a flower doesn't bloom, you fix the environment in which it grows, not the flower" (www.alexanderdenheijer.com/quotes).

Benefits of Support and Encouragement in Teams

Support and encouragement play a vital role in teacher teams, offering a range of benefits that positively impact both teachers and students. Let's look at some of the benefits, including enhanced job satisfaction, increased collaboration and teamwork, improved professional growth and development, and enhanced student outcomes.

Encouraging each other can have a significant impact on teachers' morale and job satisfaction, leading to a more positive work environment. When teachers feel supported and valued by their colleagues, administrators, and the overall team, they experience an increase in motivation, engagement, and overall job satisfaction. This positive atmosphere can help reduce stress and burnout, allowing teachers to focus on their teaching responsibilities and perform at their best.

Team support fosters a culture of collaboration and teamwork within teacher teams. When teachers feel supported, they are more likely to share ideas, resources, and best practices with their colleagues. This sharing of knowledge and expertise promotes a collaborative atmosphere, where teachers work together to solve problems, develop innovative teaching strategies, and support one another. Collaborative teamwork strengthens the overall effectiveness of the team, benefiting both teachers and students.

Support and encouragement contribute to the professional growth and development of teachers. When teachers receive constructive feedback, mentorship, and encouragement from their colleagues, they are motivated to reflect on their practices, identify areas for improvement, and engage in continuous professional learning. This focus on growth and development not only enhances teachers' instructional skills and pedagogical approaches; it also nurtures a culture of lifelong learning within the team.

The ultimate goal is to enhance student outcomes. When teachers feel supported and encouraged, they are more likely to create a positive and nurturing learning environment for their students. This positive environment promotes student engagement, motivation, and academic achievement. Additionally, when teachers collaborate and share resources and expertise, they can effectively differentiate instruction to meet the diverse needs of students, leading to improved student outcomes.

Honk If You . . .

Praise should be the majority of your communication. Indeed, as with geese, encouragement and praise should be a major focus of communication within a school team. Geese flying in a V formation often honk to encourage and support each other, creating a positive and motivating atmosphere. Similarly, in a school setting, incorporating encouragement and praise into communication has several benefits:

   ◆ Encouragement and praise go a long way in keeping teachers, students, and team members motivated.

When you recognize and acknowledge their efforts and achievements, it boosts their confidence and enthusiasm, inspiring them to keep pushing forward.

◆ Encouragement and praise have a direct impact on performance. When individuals feel acknowledged and valued, they are more likely to strive for excellence and give their best effort. It promotes a growth mindset and a culture of continuous improvement.

It's important to ensure that encouragement and praise are genuine and specific. Specific praise highlights the effort, progress, or unique strengths of individuals, reinforcing their positive behaviors and outcomes. Additionally, it's essential to balance praise with constructive feedback to promote growth and improvement. Just make sure the praise is significantly more common than critique. We suggest that for every criticism, there should first be five praises! By making encouragement and praise a central aspect of communication within a school team, you create an uplifting and inspiring culture that fosters motivation, confidence, positive relationships, and improved performance.

Genuine praise and encouragement help build self-confidence in individuals. This confidence extends to their abilities as educators or students, empowering them to take on challenges and reach new heights. Regularly offering encouragement and praise also fosters positive relationships within the school team. It creates a supportive and uplifting environment where everyone feels valued and appreciated. In fact, did you know that when teachers feel valued and feel like their strengths are being utilized, they are six times more engaged and effective? That's right - six times! Now that is something to honk about!

Praise can be a powerful tool for encouraging and motivating teachers, as well as facilitating a positive feedback loop. When teachers receive genuine praise for their efforts and achievements, it fosters a sense of validation and recognition, which can boost their morale and self-confidence. This in turn creates an environment where they are more open to receiving constructive feedback.

When teachers feel appreciated and acknowledged for their work, they are generally more receptive to suggestions for improvement. Positive reinforcement through praise helps establish a foundation of trust and respect between you and the teacher, making the feedback process more effective.

Additionally, frequent and genuine praise can create a positive atmosphere where strengths and successes are highlighted, leading to an increased focus on what is going well. In such an environment, the need for criticism or critique may naturally decrease, because the emphasis is on building upon existing strengths rather than solely pointing out weaknesses.

The reality is that most schools don't praise enough. Schools should be a place of praise and celebration for students and for staff. This keeps morale high and makes everyone feel valued. So, we encourage schools to fill their hallways with Honks of praise and appreciation! Let everyone know you're a team and you support each other! Honk, Honk, Honk!

Shared Responsibility: Enhancing Team Morale for Improved Collaboration

Team morale is a critical factor in fostering a collaborative and productive environment within educational institutions. When team members share the responsibility of maintaining high morale, it creates a positive atmosphere that enhances collaboration, innovation, and overall effectiveness. In this article, we will explore the concept of shared responsibility for team morale and discuss strategies to improve collaboration within educational teams.

Shared responsibility refers to the collective ownership of team morale by each member of the educational team. It involves recognizing that every individual's attitude, actions, and contributions impact the overall team morale. By embracing shared responsibility, team members understand that they have the power to influence and shape the team's culture and atmosphere.

Effective communication is the cornerstone of any successful team. Encourage team members to engage in open and respectful dialogue, actively listen to one another, and share ideas and concerns. Establish regular team meetings or forums where everyone can contribute and have their voices heard. By promoting a culture of positive communication, team members will feel valued, understood, and motivated to collaborate.

Collaboration is the lifeblood of educational teams. Foster an environment that encourages collaboration by emphasizing the value of collective problem-solving and decision-making. Encourage team members to seek diverse perspectives, share expertise, and work together toward common goals. Emphasize the idea that the team's success depends on the collective effort of all members.

Acknowledging and appreciating each team member's contributions is essential for boosting morale and promoting collaboration. Create a culture of recognition by celebrating achievements, both large and small. Encourage team members to show appreciation for one another's work and provide constructive feedback. Recognize that every individual brings unique strengths to the team and ensure that these contributions are acknowledged and valued.

Investing in the professional growth of team members demonstrates a commitment to their success and well-being. Provide opportunities for professional development, such as workshops, conferences, or mentoring programs. Encourage team members to pursue continuous learning and offer support in their career advancement endeavors. By fostering a culture of growth and development, team members will feel empowered and motivated, leading to improved collaboration.

Creating a positive work environment is crucial for enhancing team morale. Encourage team members to foster positive relationships, promote mutual respect, and support one another. Address conflicts or issues promptly and transparently, ensuring that all voices are heard and concerns are addressed. Foster a sense of belonging and inclusion within the team, valuing diversity and embracing different perspectives.

Improving team morale and collaboration in educational settings requires a shared responsibility among team members. By fostering positive communication, encouraging collaboration, recognizing and valuing contributions, supporting professional growth, and nurturing a positive work environment, educational teams can create a culture that enhances morale and drives collaboration. Remember, when each team member takes ownership of team morale, the collective impact can be transformative, leading to improved outcomes and a more fulfilling educational experience for all.

 ## Sharpen Your Winning Edge

1. Name your "what ifs" and then discuss your "how-tos," and make change happen!
2. Teacher Spotlight Podcasts or Interviews: Start a podcast or interview series where teachers are featured and celebrated for their expertise, innovative teaching methods, or unique experiences. This allows teachers to share their insights and inspire others.
3. Have a "honk" board and let staff fill out encouragement cards about a colleague when they observe something positive about them.

8

Principle 8: The Power of Transparent Communication: Fostering Trust within School Communities

One of my favorite movies of all time is the film *Remember the Titans* (2000), directed by Boaz Yakin. The movie tells the story of a high school football team overcoming racial tensions and building unity.

The locker room is filled with tension as players from different racial backgrounds, initially divided and distrustful, prepare for a crucial football game. Coach Boone (played by Denzel Washington), a determined and strong-willed leader, steps forward to address the team:

COACH BOONE: All right, listen up! We've got one shot to make this team work. And I don't care if you're black, white, or purple. We are one team, one heartbeat. But to get there, we need open and honest communication. We need to understand each other, respect each other, and have each other's backs.

The players exchange skeptical glances, unsure of how this will unfold.

COACH BOONE: So I want each one of you to look your teammate in the eye and tell them something you appreciate

DOI: 10.4324/9781003453819-9

about them. No holding back, no judgment. Let's build trust right here, right now.

The players begin to pair up, some reluctantly, while others embrace the challenge.

> PLAYER 1, a white player, locks eyes with PLAYER 2, an African American player.
>
> PLAYER 1: (earnestly) I appreciate your speed and agility on the field. You make us better.
>
> PLAYER 2: (sincerely) Thanks, man. And I appreciate your dedication and never giving up, even when things get tough.

The scene continues with various players expressing their appreciation for one another, crossing racial boundaries, and building connections.

The team gathers on the football field, their newfound trust and unity evident in their actions.

COACH BOONE: Remember, we're not just playing for ourselves. We're playing for each other, for this team. We've come a long way, but we still have a long way to go. Let's show them what we're made of!

The team takes the field, united and determined, ready to face their opponents and overcome the odds.

This scene showcases how open and honest communication can bridge divides and build trust within a team. By encouraging teammates to express their appreciation for one another, Coach Boone creates a space for vulnerability and understanding. The players begin to see each other as individuals with unique strengths, fostering empathy and teamwork. Through this process, trust is built, allowing the team to overcome their differences and work together toward a common goal.

The Power of Open and Honest Communication in Building Trust

Effective communication serves as the bedrock of any prosperous organization, and educational institutions are no exception.

Within a collaborative school setting, the presence of open and sincere communication assumes a pivotal role in fostering trust among all members of the community, including educators, administrators, support staff, and students. Transparent communication not only promotes comprehension and minimizes misunderstandings but also cultivates a culture of trust and reverence. This chapter delves into the importance of open and honest communication in establishing trust within a school community, while offering practical approaches for teachers to inspire and implement this vital practice.

A fundamental aspect of fostering trust through open and honest communication lies in acknowledging the significance of creating an environment where every individual feels heard, respected, and valued. By facilitating the exchange of ideas, concerns, and feedback, open and sincere communication leads to enhanced comprehension and collaboration. When individuals are granted the freedom to express themselves candidly and transparently, trust flourishes, nurturing stronger relationships and fostering a positive school ethos.

Active listening stands as another indispensable element of open and honest communication. As an educator, you can enhance your listening skills by wholeheartedly focusing on the speaker, maintaining unwavering eye contact, and displaying genuine interest. Through active listening, you convey your regard for the speaker's perspective, thereby fostering a sense of trust and validation.

Transparency in communication plays a pivotal role in cultivating trust. Endeavor to convey information in a lucid, concise, and timely manner. Share pertinent updates, disseminate school policies and decisions, and promptly communicate vital information. When individuals have access to accurate and up-to-date information, trust in the decision-making process and the overall school community is fortified.

Promote an atmosphere where questions and feedback from all members of the school community are encouraged. Establish platforms for sharing ideas, such as suggestion boxes or regular feedback sessions, which demonstrate that every voice is valued and considered. Foster an open dialogue where individuals feel at ease expressing their opinions and providing constructive feedback.

Address conflicts and misunderstandings promptly and constructively. Conflict resolution forms an integral part of open and honest communication. Ensure that all parties involved have the opportunity to express their perspectives and collaborate on finding a resolution. By fostering open dialogue and facilitating resolution, trust can be built, and positive relationships can be maintained within the school team.

As an educator, you play a vital role in modeling open and honest communication for your students and colleagues. Demonstrate active listening, engage in respectful dialogue, and uphold transparency in your own communication practices. By exemplifying these behaviors, you inspire trust and encourage others to follow suit.

Embrace technology as a means of communication. In today's digital age, technology offers myriad channels for effective communication. Utilize email, online platforms, and communication apps to facilitate open and transparent communication among colleagues, administrators, and parents. Embracing technology streamlines communication processes and ensures that important information reaches all stakeholders in a timely and accessible manner.

Building trust is an ongoing process. Regularly reflect on your communication practices and seek feedback from colleagues, administrators, and students. By continuously evaluating and improving your communication skills, you foster an environment of trust and collaboration.

Encouraging transparent communication, practicing active listening, creating a safe environment, and embracing feedback are all essential strategies for building trust. By implementing these strategies, you can establish a solid foundation of trust, understanding, and collaboration, ultimately leading to improved student outcomes and a thriving educational environment.

The Grapevine of Distrust

The "grapevine" refers to the informal network of communication that spreads rumors, gossip, and unofficial information among teachers and staff. While the grapevine can serve as a source of information and social bonding in some cases, it can also lead to distrust among teachers for several reasons.

Inaccuracy and distortion: Information shared through the grapevine is often distorted or incomplete, as it passes through multiple individuals. Rumors can be exaggerated, misinterpreted, or entirely false, leading to misunderstandings and a lack of trust in the information being circulated.

Lack of transparency: The grapevine bypasses formal channels of communication, such as official announcements or direct conversations. When teachers receive important information through unofficial sources, they may feel excluded or perceive a lack of transparency from the rest of the team. The grapevine tends to be selective in sharing information, and certain individuals or groups may have more access to it than others. This can create a sense of favoritism or exclusion among teachers, leading to divisions and a breakdown of trust within the team.

In fact, one of the quickest ways to lose trust is for some people to be privy to information and others not to be. Holding on to knowledge is the currency of the unproductive. These are the people who only have value because of the secrets they know. They do very little, but people are afraid of them because of what they know. You may have experienced a situation with a teacher or teachers who fit this description. You wonder how they keep their job because they seem so negative and don't do a great job in the classroom, but they seem to know all the gossip and confidential information that the rest of the staff is not privy to. I remember a teacher like this, and she let everyone know that they better not get on her bad side. People often joked that she must have the goods on the administration. There were times when she seemed to almost antagonize some teachers and even some administrators. It was a very toxic culture, simply because there was a lack of transparency that permeated the school.

This distrust can breed negativity. Gossip and rumors often thrive on the grapevine, and negative information or speculation about colleagues, administrators, or policies can circulate rapidly. This constant exposure to negativity can foster a toxic environment and damage trust among teachers, as they may feel that their colleagues or superiors are not supportive or trustworthy.

When the grapevine becomes the primary source of information, it can undermine the credibility of official communication channels. Teachers may question the accuracy or relevance of official announcements if they have become accustomed to relying on unofficial sources, further eroding trust in the organization's communication processes.

Dealing with the grapevine within a team of teachers requires a proactive and strategic approach to foster open communication and mitigate the spread of rumors and misinformation. To address the grapevine effectively, it is crucial to establish a culture of trust, transparency, and collaboration. Open and honest communication channels should be emphasized, where teachers feel encouraged to share information, concerns, and ideas directly with one another.

Regular team meetings and clear, timely communication from official sources can help ensure that accurate information is disseminated promptly. Encouraging collaboration and peer support among teachers strengthens the bonds within the team and reduces reliance on unofficial channels for information. It is essential to address concerns and misunderstandings swiftly and directly, providing a safe space for open dialogue and resolving issues before they escalate. Leading by example as a team leader or administrator, by practicing transparent and approachable communication, sets a strong foundation for trust and encourages teachers to follow suit. By actively addressing the grapevine and fostering a culture of open communication, the team can maintain a positive and productive environment based on reliable information and trust among colleagues.

The Key Role of Consistency and Reliability

Consistency and dependability stand as pivotal qualities for a team of educators striving for triumph in the ever-evolving realm of education. When teachers consistently exhibit their dependability and faithfully fulfill their commitments, they forge trust and assurance among their colleagues, students, and stakeholders. This bedrock of trust paves the way for effective collaboration, open channels of communication, and the cultivation of a nurturing learning milieu.

One fundamental facet of fostering consistency and reliability lies in clear and transparent communication. Within the team, it becomes imperative to ensure that communication remains lucid, unwavering, and easily understood. By explicitly articulating expectations, responsibilities, and timelines, potential misunderstandings and perplexities can be averted. Regular updates regarding progress and any alterations that may impact the team's work help keep everyone well-informed and aligned.

Another vital element revolves around a steadfast commitment to meeting deadlines. Adhering to timelines and delivering on agreed-upon deliverables serves as a testament to reliability. When team members consistently meet deadlines and achieve milestones, they exemplify their unwavering dedication and accountability. Even in the face of unforeseen circumstances that may pose potential delays, proactive communication and the presentation of alternative solutions or revised timelines further bolster their commitment to reliability. For instance, consider a team of teachers collaborating on a project, with each member pledging to complete their assigned tasks within a specific deadline. They consistently meet these deadlines, undeterred by unexpected challenges. If a teacher foresees a possible delay, they proactively communicate with the team, offer alternative solutions, and adjust timelines accordingly, upholding their commitment to reliability.

Dependability in collaborative endeavors also assumes paramount importance. Demonstrating reliability and dependability in team discussions, meetings, and projects entails actively contributing and actively participating. Following through on assigned tasks and responsibilities with a focus on delivering high-quality work showcases professionalism and ensures that expectations are met. Consistently showing up and engaging wholeheartedly in collaborative efforts fosters a profound sense of reliability and trust within the team.

Consistency in decision-making holds equal significance. Making decisions based on clear criteria, objective analysis, and with the best interests of the team and students at heart instills confidence in the decision-maker. Steering clear of arbitrary or erratic decisions aids in establishing a sense of reliability, fairness, and transparency within the team.

By embodying these principles of consistency and reliability, a team of educators can cultivate a culture of trust, collaboration, and efficacy. Together, they can navigate the challenges that accompany education, provide a stable and supportive environment for students, and achieve extraordinary outcomes that surpass individual endeavors (Goddard et al., 2000).

Cultivating Empathy and Support Within Teams

In a team, creating a supportive and empathetic environment is essential for fostering collaboration, building trust, and strengthening relationships. When colleagues face challenges or difficulties, it's crucial to demonstrate understanding, compassion, and a willingness to lend a helping hand. This not only provides valuable support but also contributes to a positive team culture where everyone feels valued and encouraged.

Imagine that a colleague opens up to you about their challenges or expresses their emotions. It's crucial to let them know that you understand and empathize with what they're going through. By acknowledging their experiences and validating their feelings, you create a safe space where they feel comfortable sharing and seeking support.

Respect and understanding are also vital. In a team, it's important to show respect for your colleagues' ideas, perspectives, and opinions, even if they differ from your own. Actively listen to them and engage in thoughtful conversations to better understand their viewpoints. Embrace the diversity within your team and value the unique contributions each member brings. This helps create an inclusive and collaborative environment where everyone feels respected and valued.

Being proactive in helping is another key aspect. Keep an eye out for when your colleagues face challenges or difficulties and be ready to lend a helping hand. Pay attention to their needs and offer practical support. It could be sharing relevant resources, suggesting strategies or solutions, or simply offering your time and expertise. By showing that you're there to support them and contribute to their success, you strengthen the bonds within your team.

It's also crucial to maintain the trust of your colleagues by respecting the confidentiality of their personal and professional matters. Create an environment where they feel safe about opening up without worrying about their information being shared with others. Respecting confidentiality builds stronger relationships and encourages open and honest communication within the team.

Finally, regular check-ins can make a big difference. Take the initiative to have informal conversations or scheduled meetings with your colleagues to show genuine interest in their well-being, progress, and challenges. Actively listen to their feedback, offer encouragement, and provide support where needed. Regular check-ins help foster stronger connections, build teamwork, and allow you to address any issues promptly. If the COVID pandemic has taught us anything, it is that we are all dealing with stuff. And it is so important for us to check in and check on our teammates. In fact, did you know? Geese exhibit remarkable care for injured members by forming a protective circle, adjusting flight speed, providing assistance during takeoff and landing, sharing warmth and comfort through huddling, and engaging in collective care to prevent isolation. These behaviors demonstrate their empathy, ensuring the safety and inclusion of the injured goose within the flock. When I share this in PD sessions, I like to emphasize how empathic animals can be and that sadly, they are at times more caring than some humans. Maybe we can learn more from the geese than just team building.

Be Fully Present!

I was the closing keynote speaker for the Oklahoma Association of Elementary Principals recently, and I had a principal share with me afterward that she really loved what I shared, and that one point really stuck out to her. It was about being fully present. She said that with all the multitasking a leader has to do, we do sometimes forget to be as fully present in the moment as possible.

For instance, have you ever attended a meeting and said "present" when they called your name, but then for most of the meeting, you weren't really present or at least not fully present? Or have you asked for a meeting with someone, like a colleague or even your administrator, and they spent most of their time checking their phone or preoccupied with something else?

There is a difference between being present and being fully present. This is not just true in school but in our everyday lives as well. For instance, we always like to talk about being in the moment, but the reality is that most people are only paying full attention in the present moment 50 percent of the time. That means we basically miss out on half our life, with our attention somewhere other than in the moment.

It is important to be in the moment; to be fully present with your teachers, staff, and even students. I can't tell you the number of messages I get from teachers who say they wish their admin would slow down and really listen to them. To take an extra moment in the hallway when you ask "how are you" and take time to really listen to their response. You never know what you may be missing if you are just going through the motions, or your mind is elsewhere. Leaders, when you meet with teachers and staff, make sure to set enough time aside to be fully present with them. Otherwise if you aren't fully engaged, then they feel you don't value them or their time when that may not be the case at all. This is true of collaborative planning time or team meetings. I know you have busy schedules, so instead of asking someone to "make it quick," just schedule a time to meet with them later. And then make sure that time is solely focused on them. None of us like when you are speaking to someone and they are on the phone, texting, or doing something else instead of engaging with us. Most people feel this way, so no cell phone, laptop, or anything else to distract you. Just you and them and direct eye contact and full attention. It will make them feel more valued and will help you understand the situation and make better decisions.

Being fully present, or active listening in a conversation, is a valuable skill that helps build trust and foster effective communication. Here are five keys to active listening:

- ◆ Pay Attention and Be Present: Give your undivided attention to the speaker and be fully present in the moment. Eliminate distractions and focus on the speaker's words, body language, and tone of voice. Show genuine interest by maintaining eye contact, nodding, and using other nonverbal cues to convey your engagement.

- ◆ Avoid Interrupting or Jumping to Conclusions: Resist the urge to interrupt or interject your thoughts before the speaker finishes their point. Allow them to express themselves fully and avoid making assumptions or jumping to conclusions. Instead, listen actively and let the speaker know you value their perspective by giving them the space to express themselves fully.

- ◆ Reflect and Clarify: Engage in reflective listening by paraphrasing and summarizing what the speaker has said. This shows that you are actively processing their words and trying to understand their message. Ask clarifying questions to gain further insights or fill in any gaps in your understanding. This demonstrates your genuine interest in their thoughts and helps ensure clear communication.

- ◆ Empathize and Validate: Practice empathy by trying to understand the speaker's emotions and perspective. Put yourself in their shoes and acknowledge their feelings without judgment. Validate their experiences by expressing empathy and understanding. This helps create a supportive and non-judgmental environment, which encourages open and honest communication.

- ◆ Respond Thoughtfully: When it's your turn to respond, do so thoughtfully and constructively. Use what you've gathered from active listening to provide a relevant and meaningful response. Avoid immediately shifting the focus to yourself or offering unsolicited advice. Instead, respond with empathy, understanding, and respect for the speaker's viewpoint.

By incorporating these five keys to active listening into your conversations, you can cultivate stronger connections, promote effective communication, and build trust with others. Finally, learn to be focused on the moment, whether you are at school or home. It can be easy to be on autopilot with your day-to-day schedule, but it is important to spice it up a bit each day so that you are able to actually enjoy the present. We are creatures of habit, and often when we are in the "fray of the day" we turn on autopilot and in those instances we don't fully engage. Giving your full attention means you value the people or the activities with which you are engaged. So don't just carpe diem, but carpe diem to the fullest!

Sharpen Your Winning Edge

1. Try more meaningful conversations – When you fully participate in a conversation and take the time to listen to what the other person has to say, you will always take something important away from the discussion. By giving your undivided attention and truly listening to their words, you open yourself up to new perspectives, insights, and knowledge. The next time you find yourself in a conversation, remember the power of being fully present and actively listening – the rewards are immeasurable.

2. Trust-Building Exercises: Organize trust-building exercises that require participants to work together and communicate openly. For example, try a team-building activity where participants have to solve a problem collectively, relying on effective communication and trust in one another's abilities. I remember doing rope course activities with my grade-level team, and the experience definitely helped us bond.

3. Communication Skills Inventory: Conduct a self-assessment of your communication skills and behaviors. Identify your strengths and areas for growth when it comes to open and honest communication. Set specific goals for developing and honing your communication skills to build trust more effectively. Regularly review your progress and make adjustments as needed.

9

Principle 9: Uniting Through Inclusion: Strengthening with Diversity

What does diversity mean to you? Depending on which leader or person you ask, you may get many different answers. At the same time, depending on what part of the country you are in, you may find more or less diverse staff members in terms of ethnicity, yet they are all likely to be diverse in age and experience in the field of education. Regardless of the make-up of a group, diversity enhances teamwork and problem-solving abilities.

When we hear the term diversity, we think of the presence of individuals from various backgrounds, cultures, demographics, perspectives, abilities, and experiences within a team. It encompasses differences, such as race, gender, age, ethnicity, sexual orientation, socioeconomic status, and more.

But there are also other types of diversity, often not thought of when discussing this topic. A staff could be diverse in respect to mothers and fathers. Perhaps there are grandparents on staff. Military versus non-military background. Urban versus rural upbringing. Experience in a certain position within the establishment, such as being a person who has taught their grade for 28 years give or take, versus someone fresh out of college. Even deeper, there are differences in grit, perseverance, work

DOI: 10.4324/9781003453819-10

ethic, and mindsets. How about a staff member who has stayed through multiple administrators, as opposed to someone who has never had to adapt to new leadership?

In a school that runs well, no matter the type of diversity or to what extent the term fits a staff, different thought processes are always a piece of the puzzle. Each person should be able to share their own perspective on each aspect of a team goal or expectation.

The same can be said when it comes to a professional sports team, legal team, or even a surgical team. Many may be well-versed in tried-and-true methods, whereas the newer generation may have more skill with the latest technological advances in their field.

In the movie *Moneyball*, general manager of the Oakland Athletics Billy Beane is tasked with creating a team with limited financial resources. During the beginning of the film, he is reflecting on his past and trying to find the best way to navigate the future. At one point, his team of "baseball guys" with multiple years of experience are ready to discuss the players and who they want to use to field their team in the upcoming year.

"Who do you want to discuss first, Billy?" the assistant general manager asks. They all eagerly await as Beane wages a battle within himself regarding whether he wants to go down the same path he has, or if he wants to blaze a new trail in sports. Finally, after a suspenseful pause, he makes his choice.

"None of them," he says, answering the question. And with that, he decides to go for it and usher in a new system of choosing players.

Billy Beane then writes down a player's name and announces it to his staff, who immediately respond with moans and groans about how that player isn't a good choice. The same reaction occurs for the next two players, and finally Billy starts to explain his reasoning. He also uses this moment to introduce a new member of his team, Pete, whom nobody has even met, let alone have any trust or relationship with.

We hear him say, "He gets on base, Rocco! Do I care if it is a hit or a walk?" He then snaps his fingers (which is Pete's cue to answer).

"No, he does not," Pete says, answering the question.

This new member of the team is not a "baseball guy" per se. He is a statistician who uses analytics to determine the most efficient way to find 25 players who will make the best team in baseball, at the lowest price (which Billy needed). He shows them a diverse way of thinking. A new thought process. In the end, it was about taking the right people to create the best team possible given their constraints.

When we look at geese, they are no different than the staff at a school, or a staff taking the field as a baseball team. First, they are all geese with the ability to do the job, just as the staff at a school are all educators with training and talent, or a group of players are all athletic humans with the ability to play a game. Second, they all have the goal of being the best they can be to meet the expectations of those around them. Third, they depend on each other. Without the entire team, the group is not a whole; it's just individual parts. Finally, there is diversity in their group. The team of geese ranges in strength, size, experience, knowledge, determination, work ethic, and being team players, just as discussed earlier in this chapter.

We can go back to the very beginning of the book and look at our two characters, Cole and Harry, as an example of two very diverse individuals who come together for a common goal. Harry is a good ol' boy from the South, who knows about racing and moonshine and has been involved with NASCAR for years. Cole is from California and has no experience with NASCAR, or really even with people from the south, but he can drive a car. Two humans, same interest in winning races, two very different backgrounds. Yet they eventually find a way to use their differences to create a team that wins.

The diversity is more than just ethnicity. It is every difference of the entire group, no matter the characteristic. With these differences comes the ability to create the best teams possible. When a team is full of robots, it may be efficient, but it would not have the ability to problem-solve if a storm came up in their path.

The importance of inclusive practices in creating a cohesive team is paramount to creating success. Teams must embrace their diversity, their differences, and use them to meet their potential, not point them out for negative reasons. It is why the pitcher isn't the catcher. Or why the best reliever closes the game to secure the win instead of hitting ninth in the line-up. The diversity of ability is why certain individuals on the legal team provide the closing arguments. It is also why certain surgeons are the ones to complete the heart transplant in the operating room.

Schools are no different, and leaders need to place their people in positions where they can be most successful for the team. Those who are good at numbers can help with data disaggregation. Those with backgrounds similar to the students can create relationships with students of the same background to promote successful ways to grow as humans and assist when facing adversity that they themselves may have faced in their past.

Regardless of your stature or position within an organization, everyone should be able to listen to and respect diverse perspectives and agree that the best answer may not be their perspective when facing an issue or working to implement a new system for success.

Geese exemplify how to use diversity as a strength. The diverse backgrounds and strengths of geese in a flock allow them to come together as a group and survive their journey and the challenges they face. In the end, they do not care what characteristics each goose may possess. They care that it can help the team and get them to their destination. It doesn't matter what goose honks; the leader of the V formation listens and takes the communication into account, because all communication is based upon each bird's diverse perspective. What you have in the end is a group of geese, all different in many ways, using their diversity as a strength, all working toward a common goal, regardless of their background or differences. What you have is a team.

A leader's job is not to have the best idea; it is to make sure that the best idea gets used. But to do that, the leader does have the responsibility of making sure the right people are in the room where the ideas are being put on the table. This is what we saw with Billy Beane earlier. He had his best people in the room, but he made sure the right person (Pete) had a seat at the table as well. A leader must ensure that the right perspectives are available to the team so that the best outcome can be achieved. A person who has never set foot on a campus should not be invited onto the campus to make a big decision unless many people who have been on campus are there as well, to ensure that any decisions made are the best for the people they will affect. There cannot be a decision made for the kindergarten team without kindergarten teachers at the table.

Billy Beane's team, the Oakland As, marches down this new path of analytics set forth by their leader, on a trail that was created by the new guy, Pete, and, through the use of clear communication and multiple V principles, end up setting the Major League record for consecutive wins in a row (20). The person who hit the home run to put them into the record books was one of the first three players the staff argued about in that first meeting, which was a poetic way of signifying that embracing a diverse thought from someone who had a different background or different viewpoint put them on the right path to success.

Benefits of Diversity

Diversity is a powerful catalyst that transforms school teams into vibrant hubs of learning and growth. When individuals from various backgrounds, cultures, and perspectives come together, the learning experience becomes enriched and dynamic. So, let's explore how diversity within school teams enhances the learning process, improves problem-solving abilities, encourages creativity and innovation, prepares students for a globalized world, and fosters the development of inclusive communities. By embracing diversity, students also gain the skills necessary to thrive in an increasingly diverse and interconnected world, fostering personal growth and contributing to a brighter future.

Diversity within a school team has a profound impact on the learning experience and the creation of inclusive communities. When students from diverse backgrounds, cultures, and perspectives come together, it creates a dynamic environment where they can engage in meaningful discussions, challenge their biases, and broaden their understanding of different viewpoints. This diversity enhances the learning process, fosters critical thinking, empathy, and prepares students for the interconnected world they will face.

One significant advantage of having a diverse school team is the improvement in problem-solving abilities. The inclusion of members with diverse backgrounds and experiences brings a range of problem-solving strategies and approaches to the table. This diversity of thought enables the team to generate more innovative and comprehensive solutions to challenges. By considering multiple viewpoints, students can identify blind spots and develop well-rounded solutions that incorporate various perspectives.

Moreover, diversity fuels creativity and innovation within school teams. When students collaborate with peers who have different perspectives, they are exposed to a wider range of ideas and approaches. This diversity of thought ignites creativity, encouraging students to think outside the box, question conventional wisdom, and come up with novel solutions to problems. By embracing diverse perspectives, students unlock their creative potential and contribute to a more innovative learning environment.

In today's interconnected and globalized world, it is essential for students to develop cultural competence and adaptability. Interacting with diverse team members exposes students to different cultures, languages, customs, and traditions, fostering cultural awareness, sensitivity, and respect. This exposure prepares students to navigate the diverse workplaces and communities they will encounter in the future. By embracing diversity, schools equip students with the necessary skills to thrive in a global society where connections and interactions are increasingly diverse.

The benefits of diversity within school teams are extensive. It promotes a rich learning environment, enhances problem-solving abilities, stimulates creativity and innovation, prepares students for a globalized world, and fosters the development of inclusive communities. By embracing diversity, schools empower students with the skills necessary to thrive in an increasingly diverse and interconnected world. The power of diversity is a driving force that propels schools toward excellence and creates opportunities for a brighter future.

Promoting Inclusivity

Creating an inclusive and supportive team environment is crucial for fostering collaboration, promoting growth, and maximizing the potential of every team member. In order to achieve this, it is essential to implement strategies that prioritize open communication, collaboration, professional development, diversity recognition, and conflict resolution. These strategies work together to create a team culture that values inclusivity, encourages active participation, and supports the diverse perspectives and experiences of each team member.

Fostering open communication is fundamental to creating an environment where team members feel comfortable expressing their thoughts, concerns, and ideas. By actively listening and valuing each team member's perspective, a sense of inclusion is cultivated, enabling fruitful discussions and collaboration. Open communication paves the way for sharing knowledge and experiences, creating a deeper understanding and appreciation of the diverse viewpoints within the team.

Promoting collaboration and teamwork further strengthens the inclusive team dynamic. Encouraging team members to work together, share knowledge, and support one another creates a sense of unity and shared purpose. Collaboration not only enhances problem-solving and decision-making but also ensures that each team member's contributions are valued, fostering a culture of inclusivity and empowerment.

To ensure your teachers are equipped with the necessary tools and knowledge, providing professional development and training focused on cultural competence and inclusivity is crucial. By offering opportunities for growth and learning, teachers can develop the skills to create an inclusive learning environment that meets the diverse needs of their students. Training on topics such as unconscious bias and inclusive teaching practices empowers teachers to embrace diversity and promote inclusivity in their classrooms.

Recognizing and celebrating diversity within the team is another essential aspect of fostering inclusivity. Acknowledging the diverse backgrounds, cultures, and experiences of team members creates a sense of appreciation and respect. Creating opportunities for teachers to share and learn about each other's cultures and traditions promotes understanding, breaks down barriers, and strengthens the bonds within the team.

Finally, addressing conflicts and resolving issues proactively is vital for maintaining an inclusive team environment. By dealing with conflicts or misunderstandings promptly and respectfully, a supportive atmosphere is maintained, and the concerns of team members are addressed. Open dialogue, mediation, and support demonstrate a commitment to inclusivity and ensure that everyone's voice is heard and valued.

And never underestimate the impact that inclusivity has on the students. Inclusiveness among teachers is immensely beneficial to students as it creates an environment where every student feels valued, accepted, and supported. When teachers embrace inclusiveness, students are more likely to engage actively in their learning, ask questions, and share their perspectives. This fosters a positive and collaborative classroom environment, enhancing the overall learning experience. Inclusive teachers also appreciate and celebrate the diversity of their students, promoting understanding and respect for different cultures, backgrounds, and abilities. This cultivates empathy, tolerance, and global awareness in students, preparing them to thrive in a diverse and interconnected world. Additionally, an inclusive approach to teaching ensures that every student's unique learning needs are met, leading to improved academic performance and increased self-confidence. By prioritizing inclusiveness, teachers play a crucial role in nurturing the holistic development of their students, fostering a sense of belonging, and equipping them with the skills necessary for success in both academic and personal endeavors.

Sharpen Your Winning Edge

1. Have each individual write down one characteristic that makes them unique to the school. Take your biggest issue from the chapter on the "Blame Game" and find a way to

   make those differences help you to eliminate that same issue.

2. List the five tasks that take up the majority of your day. Then prioritize them in order of importance and which gives you the most return on your investment of time. Work to find ways to eliminate the ones that are not worth your effort in order to be more efficient.

3. Open and Transparent Communication: Foster a culture of open and transparent communication by regularly sharing important information, updates, and decisions with teachers. Actively listen to teachers' concerns, ideas, and feedback and respond in a timely and respectful manner. Hold regular staff meetings or forums where teachers can voice their opinions and contribute to the decision-making process.

10

Principle 10: Elevating Leaders: Fostering Growth and Empowerment Among Teachers

Fly Away Home is a 1996 film based on the true story of Bill Lishman, a Canadian inventor, artist, and pilot who successfully trained a group of geese to follow his ultralight aircraft during their migration. Lishman used this method to help guide the geese to a new winter habitat. Although the movie is based on Bill's life, Anna Paquin played the protagonist, Amy, in the movie.

In the film, Amy rescues a group of abandoned goose eggs and raises the goslings as her own. As the goslings grow, Amy realizes that they need to learn to fly and migrate to a safer habitat. However, geese are instinctually programmed to follow a lead goose.

Amy takes on the role of the lead goose, using the ultralight aircraft to guide the geese on their journey. Through patience, perseverance, and understanding the natural instincts of the geese, Amy leads them to develop their flying skills and follow her guidance.

This story highlights the importance of leadership that empowers others rather than controlling or commanding them. Amy's leadership style involves understanding the geese's

DOI: 10.4324/9781003453819-11

innate instincts and providing them with the necessary guidance and support to discover and develop their own abilities.

The story suggests that effective leadership is not just about exerting authority, but also about inspiring and enabling others to reach their full potential. By understanding and respecting the unique qualities of those being led, a true leader can foster growth, independence, and collective achievement.

Guiding Teams to Excellence

In the movie, one important takeaway is that true leadership is about guiding others to discover their own strengths and abilities. This concept can be applied in various contexts, including educational institutions. As a visionary leader in an educational institution, your role is crucial. You have the responsibility of guiding your team toward excellence by embodying certain qualities and employing specific strategies.

First, effective leaders understand that everyone possesses unique strengths and abilities. They create an environment that encourages personal growth, self-discovery, and the exploration of individual talents. You should recognize and appreciate the diverse strengths and abilities of your staff and provide opportunities for them to develop and showcase their skills.

In addition, you should provide vision and direction to your team. Craft a compelling vision statement that reflects the aspirations and goals of the school community. By articulating this vision and communicating it clearly, you inspire your team to work collectively toward a common purpose.

Guidance and support are also crucial aspects of leadership. Take the time to understand the strengths, weaknesses, and professional aspirations of your staff. Offer mentorship and professional development opportunities that align with their goals, fostering a sense of personal and professional growth. By investing in your team's development, you cultivate a motivated and engaged workforce.

Effective communication and coordination are essential for a cohesive and productive team. Establish open lines of communication with your staff, encouraging transparency and active listening. Regularly scheduled meetings, both individual and collective, provide opportunities for feedback, brainstorming, and collaboration. Utilize technology and other tools to streamline communication processes, ensuring efficient information flow throughout the team.

You bear the responsibility of creating a safe and secure environment for the entire school community. Develop and implement robust safety protocols and emergency preparedness plans, ensuring the physical well-being of students, staff, and visitors. Additionally, establish policies that promote inclusivity, respect, and a sense of belonging, fostering an emotionally safe space for all.

Motivation and encouragement play a vital role in inspiring your team to excel. Recognize and celebrate individual and collective achievements, reinforcing a culture of positivity and appreciation. Foster a supportive environment where challenges are viewed as opportunities for growth, and failures are seen as stepping stones to success. Lead by example, displaying a strong work ethic and a genuine passion for education, thereby motivating your team to emulate your dedication.

In conclusion, true leadership involves guiding others to discover their own strengths and abilities. You can successfully lead your team to success by providing vision and direction, offering guidance and support, fostering communication and coordination, ensuring protection and safety, and inspiring motivation and encouragement. By cultivating an environment conducive to growth and success, you empower your team to reach new heights and make a lasting impact on the lives of students and the broader school community.

Building a Culture of Leadership and Empowerment

In the challenging world of school administration, the weight of responsibility can often feel overwhelming. As an administrator, it's natural to feel the need to be involved in every decision, considering that the ultimate responsibility rests on your shoulders. However, it is crucial to acknowledge that this approach can contribute to perpetuating a cycle of high turnover and burnout among principals and administrators. Expecting administrators to single-handedly turn around a school, improve test scores, and boost morale is a recipe for disaster, rather than fostering a dynamic school culture.

Furthermore, even when administrators are willing to provide opportunities for leadership, there is a tendency for them to expect teachers to execute tasks in the same manner they would. Unfortunately, this unintentionally leads to micromanagement, as administrators strive to ensure that everything is done exactly as they would do it. This micromanaging approach can hinder the growth and autonomy of teachers, stifling their creativity and potential.

To counteract these challenges and foster a culture of leadership and empowerment, it is essential to give team members genuine responsibility and authority. Effective leaders understand the value of developing and empowering their followers, recognizing that teachers are the most valuable asset that the school possesses. Gallup research reveals that people who feel their strengths are utilized in their job are more engaged and have a higher quality of life. However, two-thirds of workers feel that their strengths are not fully utilized, leading to disengagement, reduced productivity, and a diminished sense of well-being.

Imagine if two-thirds of your teachers felt their strengths were fully utilized. The levels of engagement and productivity that would permeate the school would be palpable. In a faculty of teachers, such an environment would transform the entire school community. Just as children are motivated when their strengths are recognized and leveraged, adults are motivated in the same way. Focusing solely on areas of weakness or improvement can never truly intrinsically motivate individuals. However, when their talents and strengths are emphasized, motivation becomes inevitable. Research shows that people are nearly 100 percent engaged in their jobs when their administration or leaders focus on their strengths.

Unfortunately, Gallup reports that around seven out of ten teachers are "not engaged" or "actively disengaged" in their work, thus are emotionally detached from their work environment. This has significant implications for both students and administrators, since teacher engagement is the top predictor and driver of student engagement.

To address disengagement and promote retention, it is crucial to provide growth opportunities for staff members. Engage in conversations with your team about their personal vision. Do they aspire to administration or other leadership roles? Are they interested in pursuing professional growth through avenues such as becoming published authors? Let them know that you support their goals and are committed to helping them succeed.

Effective leadership is about empowering employees to take ownership of their personal productivity and self-improvement. This entails providing them with the necessary tools, training, and resources, assigning tasks based on their strengths, and setting clear goals and expectations. It also involves offering feedback, coaching, and ongoing support, ensuring that tutorials, peer mentoring, and additional training are readily available.

Effective leaders establish these steps and processes while expecting productivity, without insisting that tasks be done the same way they would do them, as micromanagement stifles effectiveness.

Ultimately, strengthening your staff's competence and confidence is paramount. Before every interaction, ask yourself how you can make individuals feel more confident, capable, and self-determined. Act on those answers, consistently developing and motivating others. To effectively develop a team of leaders, consider the following steps:

1. Delegate early: Delegate tasks in advance to alleviate unnecessary pressure, allowing sufficient planning and adjustment time.
2. Select the right person: Assess your staff's skills and capabilities, assigning tasks to the most suitable individuals. Ensure they have the necessary training and resources to succeed.
3. Communicate the rationale and benefit: Clearly explain the purpose of the task and how it contributes to the

school or team's goals. Highlight how the delegated responsibility can benefit the person, such as developing specific skills for career advancement.

4. Delegate the entire task to one person: Grant the individual complete responsibility, increasing motivation and accountability while avoiding ambiguity in accountability.

5. Set clear goals and expectations: Be specific about what is expected, providing information on what, why, when, who, and where. Leave the "how" open for their input, while confirming and verifying goals and expectations.

6. Delegate responsibility and authority: Ensure the subordinate has the necessary responsibility and authority to complete the task. Allow them to approach the task in their preferred manner, as long as the results align with your specifications. Be open to their ideas on task fulfillment.

7. Provide support, guidance, and instructions: Direct subordinates to the resources they may need, whether it's coordinating with others, accessing crucial information, or offering yourself as a resource.

8. Take a personal interest in task progress: Stay informed about the task's progress and offer assistance when necessary, maintaining open communication channels. Regular meetings for significant tasks provide ongoing feedback.

9. If progress is unsatisfactory, don't immediately reclaim the project: Instead, continue working with them to ensure they understand the task is their responsibility. Offer guidance on how to improve while ensuring accountability and dependability.

10. Evaluate and recognize performance: Evaluate results more than methods, identifying areas of improvement for better performance. Recognize successes promptly.

Allowing your staff opportunities to contribute to your vision's success is the ultimate confidence boost and empowerment. Influencing your team is the most important aspect of your job, as it holds the potential for the greatest impact. When your team feels trusted, respected, supported, and appreciated, their dedication knows no bounds.

Soaring to Excellence Through a Shared Vision

Just like the title of the book says, the power of geese is all about flying in a V formation. When geese migrate, they fly together in this special formation to save energy and reach their destination efficiently. This formation represents their shared vision of conserving energy, flying efficiently, staying safe, and communicating effectively.

By flying in this synchronized pattern, they reduce wind resistance and save energy. They also stay on course and know where they're going. The formation helps them see predators and obstacles, keeping the whole flock safe. This natural behavior shows that geese understand the importance of working together toward a common goal and increasing their chances of a successful migration.

Collaboration is just as important for effective teaching teams. A shared vision is like a catalyst for better collaboration among teachers. When teachers break down the barriers between their individual classrooms and work together toward a common goal, they create an environment where they can share ideas, strategies, and resources. They can tap into the collective wisdom of the team and benefit from each other's expertise. Collaborative planning and sharing best practices become key to professional growth and better teaching practices for all students.

Consistency in teaching is crucial for students to have a smooth learning experience. Shared goals play a big role in promoting consistency in teaching practices across the school or grade level. Teachers can align their curriculum, teaching methods, and assessments. This ensures that students receive a unified education. When there are shared expectations for what students should learn and how they should be taught, it reduces confusion and creates a clear path for students.

Ultimately, the main focus is to improve student learning. When teachers join forces with a common purpose, they can concentrate on specific areas where students need to grow and develop. They can implement targeted interventions, tailor instruction to individual needs, and use research-based strategies. Working together, teachers can identify and implement the most effective practices that support student success.

Shared goals also help teachers make the most of their resources. They can combine their resources, both human and material, to have a bigger impact on student learning. They can create a collaborative learning environment that takes advantage of each team member's strengths and talents. By developing and sharing resources like lesson plans, materials, and technology tools, they use their resources efficiently and effectively, benefiting both teachers and students.

A shared vision and goals create a supportive and united school culture where teachers feel valued. In this environment, teachers know they are part of a team working toward a common purpose. This shared vision fosters a sense of belonging, collaboration, and trust among teachers. It positively affects their well-being and job satisfaction, inspiring them to strive for excellence in their teaching practices.

Having a shared vision also helps teachers respond to new challenges and trends. Together, they can analyze the impact of changes, adjust their teaching practices, and support each other through transitions. This adaptability ensures that their teaching remains up to date, relevant, and effective at meeting the evolving needs of students.

Shared goals also hold teachers accountable for their actions and results. Teachers can track their progress toward the shared goals, reflect on their practices, and make informed decisions based on data. This sense of accountability promotes a culture of excellence and professionalism. Teachers take ownership of their professional growth and contribute to the collective success of the team.

A shared vision provides a sense of direction and purpose for teachers. When teachers understand and connect with the broader goals and vision of the school, they are more likely to feel motivated, engaged, and committed to their work. It gives them a sense of ownership and a clear understanding of how their efforts contribute to the overall mission of the school.

When there is alignment and coherence in the vision, it becomes easier to develop and implement strategies that support student learning and achievement. It helps create a sense of unity and shared purpose, fostering collaboration and teamwork among teachers. By embracing a shared vision, teachers unlock their collective potential, creating an environment that nurtures excellence and positively impacts students' lives.

As you step outside and catch the sound of random honking, whether from a bird or a passing vehicle, let it serve as a catalyst for positive change. Imagine witnessing a magnificent flock of birds soaring through the sky, united and uplifting one another with unwavering support. Take note of their synchronized flight formation, the unmistakable "V," a symbol of efficiency and collective progress. Allow this imagery to inspire your team, reminding them that true success lies in collaborative effort.

Embrace the spirit of geese, navigating the heavens in perfect harmony, and guide your school toward newfound achievements in every realm. Let the transition from summer to fall in the southern breeze carry with it the echoes of geese, a constant reminder of the profound impact this text has had on readers and leaders alike. Grateful for the wealth of knowledge about these magnificent creatures, may their flight forever symbolize the transformative power of unity and inspire you to soar to greater heights.

 ## Sharpen Your Winning Edge

1. Create platforms or structures, such as grade-level teams, department meetings, or professional learning communities, where teachers can actively contribute to decision-making and problem-solving. Empower teachers to lead initiatives or projects related to curriculum development, instructional practices, or school improvement plans.

2. Assign leadership roles and responsibilities to teachers, allowing them to take charge of specific projects, committees, or initiatives. Offer opportunities for teachers to lead professional development sessions or present at staff meetings to share their expertise and insights with colleagues.

3. Like the geese rotate to the lead position, rotate leadership positions to give different teachers the chance to develop their leadership skills and broaden their perspectives.

4. Schoolwide TED Talks: Host a schoolwide TED Talks event where teachers have the opportunity to share their vision and ideas through short, inspirational presentations. This platform allows teachers to articulate their thoughts, engage in dialogue, and inspire each other, contributing to the collective vision of the school.

11

Principle 11: Small Teams, Big Impact: Maximizing Collaboration

In the 2001 film *Ocean's Eleven*, Danny Ocean, portrayed by George Clooney, leads a team of highly skilled criminals in an intricate plan to simultaneously rob three prominent Las Vegas casinos.

The scene unfolds as each team member assumes their position and carries out their specialized role. With unique skill sets, they each play a vital part in the success of the ambitious heist. Despite the intricacy of the plan and the high stakes involved, the team members display remarkable coordination, trust, and synergy.

As the heist progresses, the scene cuts between different team members, showcasing their individual tasks and the challenges they face. From cracking safes and disabling security systems to manipulating casino staff and executing distractions, each member's contribution is crucial to the overall success of the operation.

Throughout the sequence, the power of teamwork and synchronized execution is evident. The team members communicate seamlessly and rely on each other's expertise, demonstrating a deep understanding of their roles and responsibilities. They anticipate one another's moves and adapt swiftly to unforeseen circumstances, showcasing their ability to think on their feet and collaborate effectively under pressure.

The strength of the small team becomes apparent as they overcome obstacles, outsmart security measures, and stay ahead

DOI: 10.4324/9781003453819-12

of their adversaries. Their unity and coordination enable them to conquer seemingly insurmountable challenges, turning the odds in their favor.

By the conclusion of the heist, the team members regroup and celebrate their triumph, underscoring the power of collective efforts. The scene highlights the fact that a small team of skilled individuals, working cohesively and leveraging their unique strengths, can achieve remarkable outcomes that would be unattainable for individuals working in isolation.

While it's important to note that we do not suggest activities such as bank heists, the movie emphasizes the significance of collaboration, trust, and complementary skills. It showcases how pooling talents and resources within a small team can accomplish extraordinary feats that a larger group may struggle to achieve.

Collaborative Small Teams

Collaboration has gained significant importance in the realm of education, as it facilitates the exchange of knowledge, resources, and innovative concepts to elevate student learning outcomes. To foster this collaborative spirit, the formation of small teams within educational institutions has emerged as a potent approach. These teams bring together educators who share responsibilities, interests, or expertise, allowing them to collectively strive toward common objectives. In the following sections, we will delve into several examples of small teams commonly found in schools, shedding light on their specific areas of focus and functions.

Grade-Level Teams consist of teachers who instruct the same grade level, whether it be kindergarten or fifth grade. These teams collaborate across various crucial domains such as curriculum planning, instructional strategies, and initiatives that cater to the specific needs of their grade-level students. By aligning their efforts, grade-level teams ensure a harmonious and consistent educational experience, promoting continuity and progression in the learning process.

Subject Area Teams are composed of teachers specializing in specific subjects like English language arts, math, science, or social studies. These teams work closely together to align their curricula, share valuable resources, develop standardized assessments, and engage in discussions on effective instructional practices within their respective subject areas. Through such collaboration, subject area teams guarantee vertical and horizontal alignment of content, fostering a deeper comprehension of subject-specific concepts and promoting coherence in student learning across different grade levels.

Professional Learning Communities (PLCs) serve as collaborative teams bringing together educators from various grade levels and subject areas. PLCs provide a platform for regular meetings, enabling educators to discuss student data, analyze instructional techniques, and collectively strive toward enhancing teaching and learning practices. PLCs often concentrate on specific goals, such as improving literacy instruction or implementing inquiry-based science lessons. Through ongoing professional dialogue and reflection, educators within PLCs can enhance their teaching methods and provide mutual support in achieving their shared objectives.

Intervention or Support Teams consist of teachers, specialists, and support staff who collaborate to offer targeted interventions and assistance to students who are struggling academically. These teams develop personalized intervention plans, closely monitor student progress, and adapt instructional strategies to meet the unique needs of students requiring additional support. Through their collaborative efforts, intervention or support teams ensure that every student receives the necessary assistance to thrive both academically and holistically.

Special Education Teams encompass special education teachers, general education teachers, related service providers, and administrators. These teams collaborate to develop Individualized Education Programs (IEPs), implement accommodations and modifications, and ensure the inclusion and success of students with disabilities. By pooling their expertise and resources, special education teams create an inclusive and supportive learning environment that caters to the distinctive requirements of every student.

STEM Teams bring together teachers from diverse subject areas to integrate Science, Technology, Engineering, and

Mathematics concepts and practices into the curriculum. These interdisciplinary teams promote collaboration, project-based learning, and the integration of technology and engineering principles. By working collectively, STEM teams cultivate critical thinking, problem-solving skills, and creativity among students, preparing them for success in the fields of science and technology.

School Leadership Teams encompass administrators, teachers, and staff members who collaborate to make informed decisions and shape the overall direction of the school. These teams focus on initiatives for school improvement, policy development, and the cultivation of a positive and inclusive school culture. Through their collective expertise and shared vision, school leadership teams provide guidance and support to ensure the continuous growth and success of the entire school community.

In conclusion, the establishment of small teams within educational institutions facilitates collaboration, encourages the sharing of best practices, and enhances educational outcomes. Grade-level teams, subject area teams, PLCs, intervention or support teams, special education teams, STEM teams, and school leadership teams all play pivotal roles in creating a collaborative and dynamic learning environment. By leveraging the collective expertise and resources of these teams, educators can have a profound impact on student learning, foster their professional growth, and cultivate a culture of collaboration and excellence within their respective schools.

The Benefits of Collaboration: Small Teams Enhancing Education

Collaboration among educators in small teams within the field of education brings many benefits that greatly impact curriculum alignment, the exchange of best practices, student support, professional development, and ultimately, student learning outcomes. This section explores the advantages of collaboration within small teams, highlighting its role in improving curriculum alignment, facilitating the sharing of expertise and effective methodologies, enhancing student support and individualization, promoting professional growth and introspection, and ultimately leading to improved student learning outcomes. By recognizing and harnessing the potential of small teams, educators can create a dynamic and supportive learning environment that maximizes student achievement.

Collaboration among educators significantly enhances the effectiveness of curriculum alignment. By working together, teachers at the same grade level or subject area can analyze and map their curriculum to ensure a smooth progression of content and skills. This alignment helps avoid gaps or repetitions in instruction, resulting in a more cohesive educational experience for students. Through discussions and collaboration, small teams can identify areas where concepts overlap, align assessments, and develop common pacing guides, leading to a more unified and interconnected curriculum.

Small teams provide an excellent platform for educators to share best practices and tap into their collective expertise. Within these teams, teachers can exchange innovative instructional strategies, engage in discussions about successful interventions, and share resources that have proven effective in their own classrooms. This collaborative approach exposes educators to diverse teaching methods, allowing them to adapt and incorporate fresh ideas into their teaching practices. Sharing best practices and expertise not only enhances individual teaching skills but also raises the overall quality of instruction within the team.

Collaborative teams empower educators to identify students who may be struggling and collectively develop targeted interventions and support strategies. By pooling their resources and expertise, teachers can design differentiated instruction that caters to the diverse needs of their students. Collaborative teams also provide an opportunity for educators to share successful differentiation techniques, ensuring that all students can access challenging content and reach their full potential.

Regular collaborative meetings and discussions foster reflective dialogue among teachers, enabling them to share experiences, address challenges, and celebrate successes. This collective reflection allows educators to critically analyze their teaching practices, identify areas for improvement, and develop innovative solutions. By receiving constructive feedback from their peers, teachers can refine their instructional approaches, expand their pedagogical repertoire, and continuously grow as professionals.

The ultimate goal of collaboration in education is to enhance student learning outcomes. When educators work together, leveraging their collective expertise and aligning their efforts, the impact on student achievement is significant. Through curriculum alignment, the sharing of best practices, targeted support, and continuous professional growth, small teams create an environment that promotes student success. Collaborative teams foster a cohesive and coordinated approach to instruction, resulting in increased student engagement, retention of knowledge, and academic performance.

Small teams offer numerous advantages that positively influence curriculum alignment, the exchange of best practices, student support, professional growth, and student learning outcomes. By embracing collaboration and leveraging the strengths of team members, educators can establish a transformative learning environment that maximizes student success. Encouraging and supporting collaboration within small teams should be a top priority in educational settings, as it cultivates collective excellence and contributes to a comprehensive and meaningful learning experience for all.

Strategies for Small Team Success

To ensure effective collaboration, it is important for small teams to establish shared objectives and align their goals. This creates a common vision that fosters collaboration and cohesion among team members. Clear communication channels, such as regular meetings and online platforms, play a crucial role in enabling team members to exchange ideas, discuss progress, and plan collaboratively. By sharing resources and lesson plans within the team, efficiency is promoted, workload is reduced, and creativity is stimulated. Peer observation and feedback support professional growth by allowing team members to observe each other's classrooms and provide constructive suggestions for improvement. Regular reflection sessions help the team assess their collaborative efforts, identify areas for improvement, and celebrate successes, leading to continuous improvement.

Let's consider the example of a fifth grade-level team aiming to improve student reading comprehension, which can be adapted to suit the needs of any small team.

◆ Establishing Common Goals: The fifth-grade teachers form a grade-level team with the common objective of improving students' reading comprehension skills. They focus on implementing effective reading strategies such as close reading, text analysis, and comprehension strategies to enhance students' understanding of texts. The team collaborates to develop appropriate assessments that align with their instructional goals, allowing accurate measurement of students' progress. They also recognize the importance of supporting struggling readers and implement targeted interventions such as differentiated instruction and additional reading support to address specific needs and ensure all students have an opportunity to succeed.

◆ Clear Communication Channels: The grade-level teachers establish a shared email group and a dedicated online platform to facilitate effective communication and collaboration. Through these channels, they engage in ongoing discussions, share ideas, concerns, and updates related to their grade level. This communication platform serves as a space where they can discuss instructional strategies, brainstorm innovative approaches, coordinate field trips, share important announcements with students and parents, and address any concerns or questions that arise during the school year.

◆ Regular Meetings and Collaborative Planning: The fifth-grade teachers hold weekly meetings to discuss student progress, share insights, and engage in collaborative planning. During these meetings, they review student data, analyze trends, and collectively identify areas that require additional support or adjustment in their instructional plans. They align their teaching strategies, discuss common assessments that measure reading comprehension, and address challenges or areas for improvement. Moreover, they coordinate cross-curricular activities and events to ensure a comprehensive and interconnected learning experience for their students.

◆ Sharing Resources and Lesson Plans: The grade-level teachers establish a shared Google Drive folder to support one another and promote consistency in teaching practices. Within this folder, they upload and access various resources, including lesson plans, teaching materials, activities, classroom management strategies, and parent communication templates. By sharing these resources, they create a collaborative environment where educators can draw from each other's expertise, benefit from a broader range of instructional materials, and implement effective teaching strategies. This resource sharing saves time and ensures consistency and high-quality instruction across the fifth-grade classrooms.

◆ Peer Observation and Feedback: The grade-level team implements a peer observation and feedback system to foster professional growth and improve instructional practices. Each teacher takes turns observing their colleagues' classrooms, with a specific focus on instructional practices or strategies related to reading comprehension. After the observations, they provide constructive feedback and suggestions to help refine and enhance instruction. This feedback loop encourages continuous improvement and the adoption of effective practices throughout the team. By engaging in peer observation and feedback, the teachers have the opportunity to learn from one another, refine their instructional approaches, and create an environment of collaboration and professional development.

◆ Reflection and Continuous Improvement: At the end of each grading period, the grade-level team conducts reflection sessions to evaluate their progress, analyze student data, and discuss areas of success and improvement. During these sessions, they reflect on their collaborative efforts, assess the impact of their instructional strategies on students' reading comprehension skills, and make informed decisions about adjustments or modifications needed for the next period. Setting new goals based on their reflections, the team strives for continuous improvement and ensures that they are consistently providing the best possible support for their students' reading comprehension development.

By implementing these strategies, small teams can enhance their collaboration and make significant strides toward achieving their goals.

Overcoming Challenges in Small Team Collaboration

Collaborating within a small team can bring you numerous benefits, such as fostering innovation, sharing knowledge, and cultivating a sense of collective ownership. However, small teams often encounter challenges that hinder their collaboration and effectiveness. This chapter aims to explore and provide strategies to overcome four common challenges faced in small team collaboration: time constraints and scheduling, balancing individual autonomy and team cohesion, addressing conflicting perspectives, and building trust and establishing a supportive environment. By understanding these challenges and implementing appropriate strategies, you can optimize your collaboration and achieve your goals more efficiently.

One of the primary challenges you face in small team collaboration is dealing with time constraints and scheduling conflicts. Your team members may have different schedules, commitments, or priorities, making it difficult to find common meeting times. To overcome this challenge, you can employ several strategies. First, establish a shared calendar or scheduling tool where team members can input their availability, making it easier to identify potential meeting times. Additionally, prioritize and allocate dedicated time slots for collaborative activities, ensuring that all members can commit to the scheduled meetings. Moreover, leverage technology solutions such as video conferencing and virtual collaboration platforms to mitigate time constraints, enabling remote team members to participate in meetings regardless of their physical location.

Another challenge you face is balancing individual autonomy and team cohesion within your small team. While individual autonomy promotes creativity and diverse perspectives, excessive autonomy can lead to fragmentation and a lack of alignment. To address this challenge, it is essential to establish clear team goals and expectations. Ensure that team members have a shared understanding of the team's purpose, objectives, and desired outcomes. Regular communication and feedback sessions are crucial to maintaining alignment and ensuring that individual contributions align with the team's collective vision. Furthermore, foster a culture of open dialogue and encourage active participation to strike a balance between individual autonomy and team cohesion. Respect each team member's expertise and encourage collaboration to harness the benefits of both autonomy and cohesion.

Conflicting perspectives within your small team can hinder collaboration and decision-making processes. However, diverse viewpoints can also lead to more innovative and robust solutions. To effectively address conflicting perspectives, create a safe space for open and respectful discussions. Encourage active listening and value diverse opinions to foster an environment where team members feel comfortable expressing their views. Establish ground rules for constructive dialogue, ensuring that discussions remain focused on the issues at hand rather than becoming personal. Additionally, adopt a problem-solving mindset and seek common ground to bridge differences and reach consensus. By embracing and managing conflicting perspectives effectively, you can harness the collective intelligence of your small team and make better-informed decisions.

Trust is a critical component of successful collaboration within your small team. Without trust, communication and teamwork can break down, leading to inefficiencies and reduced productivity. To build trust, actively invest in relationship building among team members. Engage in regular team-building activities, both formal and informal, to foster a sense of camaraderie and create opportunities for team members to get to know each other on a personal level. Additionally, practice open and honest communication, respect confidentiality, and honor commitments to establish trust among team members. Moreover, as a leader, set an example by being transparent, approachable, and supportive. By creating a supportive environment where team members feel valued, respected, and supported, you can cultivate trust, enhance collaboration, and achieve your collective goals.

Collaborating within a small team may present challenges, but with the right strategies and approaches, these challenges can be overcome. By addressing time constraints and scheduling conflicts, balancing individual autonomy and team cohesion, and actively managing conflicting perspectives, you can create a collaborative environment that fosters innovation and effective decision-making. Effective collaboration within small teams can lead to enhanced outcomes, improved problem-solving capabilities, and a stronger sense of unity among team members.

Sharpen Your Winning Edge

1. Learning Reflection Prompts: Provide reflection prompts or questions for educators to consider after participating in collaborative activities or team meetings. For example:
   What did I learn from this collaborative experience?
   How did my contributions impact the team's progress?
   What challenges did I encounter, and how did I over come them?
   What could I have done differently to enhance collabor ation and achieve better outcomes?

2. Collaborative Curriculum Planning: Have grade-level teams or subject area teams work together to analyze and align their curriculum. They can discuss learning

objectives, identify overlapping concepts, and develop a cohesive curriculum that ensures continuity and progression in student learning.

3. Celebrating Achievements and Milestones: Create opportunities for small teams to celebrate their achievements and milestones. Recognize and appreciate the collective efforts and successes of the team. This can foster a sense of accomplishment, boost morale, and reinforce the importance of collaboration in achieving shared objectives.

12

Principle 12: Proactive Approach to Conflict Resolution in School Teams

The hit TV show "Survivor" is a great metaphor for the entire set of "V" principles, as well as an example of every staff that assembles in August as they gear up for another school year (except they do not vote team members off the campus).

On the show, a cast of approximately 20 strangers come together on an island with a common goal: they want to be the last person remaining. Typically, members quickly form teams, which is when the "V" principles take shape (even though they are abandoned at times and in the end as selfishness and being the "sole survivor" take over).

As the season begins, the host sets the scene, discussing the goals and hopes of the journey. After introductions and discussions, teams head to their part of the island, and individuals start to feel each other out and build relationships through communication. They start to take into account the diversity of their group and assess who has skills and knowledge that will help them move forward in the game. As time goes on, trust evolves while the team adapts to the trials and tribulations of the game. They are still motivated as they work as a team and support each other during the challenges or while facing elements. They make

DOI: 10.4324/9781003453819-13

decisions based upon the needs of the group, usually for the good of the group. Through resilience and "honking" for encouragement, the teams persevere toward the finish line. As the game goes on, outcasts become identified and sometimes even sent to an island alone. At times, there can be a "Lord of the Flies" mentality, as the group eats their own in a way. The direction of the game can go either way depending on which leader takes over, and the end can be one of many possibilities.

The scenario of "Survivor" plays out in schools every year as the staff comes together in August in buildings across the world. Let's read the last paragraph through the eyes of a teacher reporting for the first day of the new year.

As the season (school year) begins, the host (leader) sets the scene, discussing the goals and hopes as the journey begins. After introductions (new teachers and support staff) and discussions (expectations or motivating videos), teams (grade levels or departments) head to their part of the island (the school building), and individuals start to feel each other out and build relationships through communication (PLC meetings). They start to take into account the diversity of their group and assess who has skills and knowledge that will help them move forward in the game. As time goes on, trust evolves while the team adapts to the trials and tribulations of the game (the school year). They are still motivated (because they are professionals) as they work as a team and support each other during the challenges (such as a behavioral challenge, difficult parent, or low test scores) while facing elements. They make decisions based upon the needs of the group (perhaps how to keep students away from each other during recess to lessen the chance of issues), usually for the good of the group. Through resilience and "honking" for encouragement, the teams persevere toward the finish line (end of the school year or teaching all the standards). As the game goes on, outcasts become identified, sometimes even sent to an island alone. At times, there can be a "Lord of the Flies" mentality, as the group eats their own in a way. The direction of the game (working through the school year) can go either way depending on which leader takes over, and the end can be one of many possibilities.

Every school year can go in many different directions and, sadly, every staff member may go into Survival mode. Nearly all teams will have to overcome adversity and team dysfunction within their time together. Many leaders will throw gas on the fires rather than using the "V" principles to adapt to issues and find solutions that work for the team.

When geese hit obstacles, they do not eat their own or create outcasts within their groups. They find a way to help each other through teamwork and communication. These have been covered in the previous chapters and when applied to a school staff, positive change will occur.

In terms of team dysfunction within a school, the group needs to attack the scenario from the viewpoint that they are working to find a solution to whatever concern has been identified. If the team can agree that they all want to fix the problem for the betterment of the team, success will occur.

But what if a member of the squad doesn't want to find an answer? In that case, the team is not being put ahead of the individual. The "independent contractor" is no longer team-oriented, and that will prevent the school from being as successful as it can be. In this case, all members of the team need to "honk" and work to help the person who is out of formation get back in formation (in a professional manner).

No matter the organization, if someone gets out of line, the "boss" is supposed to be the one who handles the discipline or discussions with that employee. The employee expects the supervisor to be the one to talk with them if there is a problem. But what if your friend or trusted colleague was also "honking" at you?

Geese all expect every other goose to honk if they are out of line in any way or dragging the team down in a negative way. If one goose is causing more resistance, the others work to help them correct it.

Schools should work in the same way. The communication is to motivate, not deflate. However, that also requires the understanding that anyone who is out of line takes the feedback and uses it in a positive way to correct behavior and improve for the good of the team.

It is important to understand that overcoming team dysfunction does not have to be done in a negative way. How school teams use these skills to overcome challenges dictates the direction of the school.

If a team takes the "honking" in a negative way, negative outcomes are going to occur. Animosity will begin; the teacher in question may be shunned within the school or by colleagues, and the culture will take a hit as they eat their own. Administration will then feel obligated to step in and work to fix the issue. Should it be too far gone, she or he will have to pick sides and eventually changes will have to be made with regards to staffing, and then even more people are affected, potentially infecting teams that once worked well.

However, if the team takes the "geese" approach to the issue and they "honk" at the person, having already established the understanding that "honking" is positive in nature and works to make the team even better, the outcomes will be vastly different. Stronger teams will grow and trust each other even more because they will know they can work together in a respectful manner, and concerns that are brought forth are done with the intent of growing the team in a positive direction.

The problem-solving and decision-making skills used by geese in flight are a model for teams within a school to use as they work to overcome the obstacles that arise during the school year. Through the use of these skills and approaches, there will not be a "sole survivor" but rather a bunch of teams who all remain on the island because they want to and enjoy their colleagues as they work to create an island paradise or, in school terms, a school where all staff stays and loves being a part of the team they have formed.

Strategies for Dealing with Challenging Teachers in a Team

Dealing with resistant teachers in a team can be a challenging task, but with effective communication and a collaborative approach, it is possible to address their concerns and foster a more positive and productive working environment. Here are some strategies you can employ to handle resistant teachers:

- ◆ Understand their concerns: Take the time to listen to the resistant teachers and understand their perspective. Identify the specific issues or reasons behind their resistance. This will help you tailor your approach and address their concerns more effectively.
- ◆ Build relationships: Establishing strong relationships based on trust and respect is crucial. Engage in open and honest conversations with the resistant teachers to build rapport. Show empathy and let them know that their opinions are valued.
- ◆ Communicate the purpose and benefits: Clearly communicate the purpose and benefits of the changes or initiatives being implemented. Explain how these changes align with the overall goals of the school or team and how they can positively impact student learning outcomes.
- ◆ Provide professional development opportunities: Offer professional development opportunities that help address the concerns of resistant teachers. Identify specific training or resources that can support them in adapting to new methodologies or approaches. This can help alleviate their resistance and empower them with the skills and knowledge needed.
- ◆ Foster collaboration: Encourage collaborative decision-making processes where teachers have a voice and can contribute to the development of plans and strategies. Seek input from resistant teachers and involve them in finding solutions. This will increase their ownership and engagement.
- ◆ Share success stories: Highlight success stories from other teachers or schools that have implemented similar changes successfully. Share evidence and data demonstrating the positive impact of the changes. This can help alleviate concerns and provide tangible examples of how the changes can be beneficial.

Proactive Approaches to Conflict Resolution

"Conflict" is a word that often evokes negative feelings and discomfort in many of us. We tend to avoid confrontation and would rather engage in almost anything else than confront another person about an issue. However, conflict is an inevitable part of life, even in the best school cultures. It is not that conflicts will never arise, but rather how we deal with them that truly matters. This is especially crucial for administrators, as one of their most important skills is the ability to handle conflict effectively.

Even geese experience conflict, but their behaviors showcase conflict resolution with their collective decision-making process. When choosing a landing site or a feeding ground, geese engage in group discussions through vocalizations and head movements. Through these interactions, they reach a consensus and make decisions that benefit the whole group, resolving potential conflicts over limited resources. The ability to handle conflict rather than ignore or avoid it helps them achieve their goals.

Effective leaders possess the skill of handling confrontations, creating an environment where teachers and staff feel safe to speak up. Teachers, by nature, are often agreeable and tend to avoid conflict, even when they know they should voice their concerns. Additionally, it is a natural human reaction to shy away from disagreeing with a superior. Therefore, administrators should recognize the significance of someone taking the risk to speak up and appreciate their courage.

Rather than shying away from conflict, administrators should see it as an opportunity to build stronger relationships with their teachers. Confrontation may be difficult because it takes us out of our comfort zone. Often, we allow issues to build up until emotions are high, leading us to overreact. However, there are strategies that can help administrators deal with conflict more effectively and transform it into a beneficial part of the communication process.

Focus on Being Proactive, Not Reactive

Reacting impulsively to conflicts rarely yields positive outcomes. For instance, if a teacher is consistently late, sending a mass email admonishing all teachers for their punctuality is unlikely to correct the specific behavior. Instead, it may negatively affect the morale of the entire staff. Proactive behavior, on the other hand, involves using sound judgment to address the issue directly. Administrators can express gratitude to the majority of teachers who consistently arrive on time, praising their commitment to punctuality. For those who are frequently tardy, individual coaching conversations can be initiated. By understanding the reasons behind their lateness, administrators can work toward finding creative solutions and ensuring their commitment to meeting expectations.

Focus on Relating, Not on Being Right

Allowing conflicts to fester often results in the focus shifting from the issue to the desire to prove oneself right. In the midst of communication, individuals may stop truly listening to one another, waiting for their turn to speak or interrupting to make their point. Administrators should remember that the goal of tough conversations is not to win arguments, but to establish a connection and reach a resolution. Relationships should take precedence over the need to be right. Relying on positional power to win an argument can create a perception of bullying, which hampers effective conflict resolution.

Focus on the Issue, Not on the Individual

Conflicts may arise due to differences in personalities rather than the actual issues at hand. It is crucial to differentiate between the two. Weak leaders may perceive strong teachers as threats, leading to conflict when these teachers express their opinions. When dealing with conflict, administrators should concentrate on addressing the behavior causing the conflict rather than attacking the personality of the individuals involved. By challenging behavior rather than the person, it becomes possible to find solutions and correct the problematic behavior without provoking defensiveness.

Focus on the Future, Not on the Conflict

Conflicts can lead to either compromise and resolution or the need for further action. Ideally, administrators should strive for compromise in resolving conflicts. However, in cases where additional steps are required, it is important to separate the issue from any personal conflicts. Teachers should understand that corrective measures are not personal attacks but a means to address problems or concerns. Administrators should emphasize that their primary focus is on resolving issues and improving the overall environment.

As we leave this section, remember that when handled well, conflict can be an opportunity for growth, learning, and improved teamwork. By implementing these strategies, teacher teams can navigate conflicts in a constructive manner, fostering a positive and productive work environment. Effective leaders understand that conflict can be a positive encounter. After all, confrontation handled well has many benefits, including:

♦ Innovative solutions to problems
♦ Improvements to the status quo
♦ Stronger confidence in implementing ideas
♦ Stronger relationships
♦ Greater harmony
♦ Improved communication
♦ Better teamwork
♦ Greater understanding
♦ Increased engagement on the job
♦ Strong passion and commitment to see success of the ideas developed

 ## Sharpen Your Winning Edge

1. Have each small group or team create a chart of "norms" for how they wish to problem solve any situation that arises within their group. Have them list items that are "understood" and will guide each discussion.
2. Schoolwide Vision Quest: Embark on a symbolic and reflective journey with teachers to explore their individual and collective aspirations for the school. Organize a vision quest, which involves a guided experience of

self-reflection, introspection, and exploration of personal values and purpose. This activity can be conducted in a natural setting, such as a park or a nearby forest, where teachers engage in activities like journaling, meditation, and group discussions. By reconnecting with their personal values and aspirations, teachers can align their individual visions with the larger shared vision of the school. The insights gained from this experience can be integrated into the school's strategic planning and decision-making processes.

3. Reverse Mentoring: Implement a reverse mentoring program where teachers can mentor administrators on topics such as technology, current educational trends, or innovative teaching methods. This approach breaks hierarchical barriers and encourages collaboration, enabling teachers to contribute their unique perspectives to shape the shared vision.

References

Goddard, R. D., Hoy, W. K., & Woolfolk Hoy, A. (2000). Collective teacher efficacy: Its meaning, measure, and impact on student achievement.
American Educational Research Journal, 37(2), 479–507.

Heathfield, S. (2016). *The 5 teams that every organization needs your
organization's needs for teams will vary but these will get you started*.
Retrieved from www.thebalancecareers.com/the-5-teams-that-
every-organization-needs-1918507

Heijer, A. Retrieved from www.alexanderdenheijer.com/quotes

Lencioni, P. (2002). *The five dysfunctions of a team*. Jossey-Bass.

Lissaman, P. B., & Shollenberger, C. A. (1970). Formation aerodynamics of
birds. *Science, 168*(3934), 1003–1005.

Rubin, R. S. (2002). Will the real SMART goals please stand up. *The
Industrial-Organizational Psychologist, 39*(4), 26–27.

Yakin, B. (Director). (2000). *Remember the Titans* [Motion picture]. Walt
Disney Pictures.

9781032592503